# LORD, LET ME GIVE YOU A MILLION DOLLARS

*Also by Dan Wooding*

Junkies Are People Too
Stresspoint
I Thought Terry Dene Was Dead
Exit the Devil (*with Trevor Dearing*)
Train of Terror (*with Mini Loman*)
Rick Wakeman, the Caped Crusader
King Squealer (*with Maurice O'Mahoney*)
Guerilla for Christ (*with Salu Daka Ndebele*)
Farewell Leicester Square (*with Henry Hollis*)
Uganda Holocaust (*with Ray Barnett*)
Miracles in Sin City (*with Howard Cooper*)
God's Smuggler to China (*with Brother David and Sara Bruce*)
Prophets of Revolution (*with Peter Aseal Gonzales*)
God's Agent (*with Brother Andrew*)

# Lord, Let Me Give You a Million Dollars

**DUANE LOGSDON**

*with Dan Wooding*

KINGSWAY PUBLICATIONS

EASTBOURNE

ISBN 0 86065 244 0

Biblical quotations are from the
Authorized Version (crown copyright).

Printed in Great Britain for
KINGSWAY PUBLICATIONS LTD
Lottbridge Drove, Eastbourne, East Sussex BN23 6NT by
Richard Clay (The Chaucer Press) Ltd, Bungay, Suffolk.
Typeset by Nuprint Services Ltd, Harpenden, Herts.

# Contents

I dedicate this book to my spiritual
father, Pastor D. Thurlow Yaxley,
whose faithfulness to the gospel, whose
love and encouragement throughout the
years, and whose expressions of love on
our spiritual birthdays, made this story
possible.

# *Foreword by Luis Palau*

Is it ever right for a minister to leave the high and holy calling of being a pastor for the apparently lesser world of business?

Is it ever God's will that a man should acquire great wealth? Should a person feel guilty for being rich even though he acquired those riches in an honourable fashion? Should he carry a cloud of guilt for the rest of his life because of this?

Can God actually use a man who leaves the ministry? Does his action grieve God's Spirit?

Duane and Carole Logsdon are a couple who faced all of these agonizing questions. Their amazing and moving pilgrimage has made this book one you will not be able to put down. In the pages ahead you will agonize with them, cry with them, and laugh with them as they struggle to face up to the demanding life of a pastor and his wife. But then you will be taken into the heart of a drama which almost shattered both of them, as they realized that God was calling them out of this ministry to do something totally unique, but also totally painful.

*Lord, Let Me Give You a Million Dollars* is a book that can change your life. Duane and Carole Logsdon are a couple who helped change mine.

*Luis Palau*
*Portland, Oregon*

# Acknowledgements

I would like first of all to thank an Englishman and an Argentinian for forgetting the differences between their two governments and being of such encouragement to both Carole and myself.

Dr Luis Palau, who was born in that South American country and is now my dear friend, plus his wife Pat, have been a great blessing to me and Carole, and I would like to thank Luis for coming up with the concept for this book.

Then I would like to thank Dan Wooding, a British author, for his untiring efforts in capturing this story in such an accurate and readable way. Also, we express our gratitude to his wife Norma, for allowing him to spend so much time away from her and their two boys, Andrew and Peter, to complete the book.

Another wonderful couple we wish to thank from the bottom of our hearts are Bill and Bettie Butler of Christian Resource Management in Orange, California. Bill 'lit the match' for this book when he first heard of it in an embryo stage, and brought in Dan Wooding to help with the writing. Then both he and Bettie, his charming wife, have spent many hours reading the manuscript and coming up with helpful suggestions to improve it.

Two vital people we must thank are Bonnie Morris, my personal secretary, who has done a great job in typing and retyping this manuscript, and also Ruth Larssen who spent many hours proofreading and typing. A big thanks to both of you.

I would also like to thank Dr Clyde Narramore for giving us the keys to transform our marriage, our very lives. He too has spent many hours checking the manuscript for us and has kindly written an epilogue for the book.

Finally, I would like to thank my pastor, Dr Chuck Swindoll of the First Evangelical Church of Fullerton, California, whose ministry has enriched our lives and helped us grow as Christians.

# CHAPTER ONE

# Eye of a Needle

'Lord, if you really want me to give up my church pastorate and go full time into the business world, please let me, in return, give you back a million dollars.'

I stopped for a moment to try and take in what I had just told the Lord. Here I was, a pastor of a successful church close to the Magic Kingdom of Disneyland in Anaheim, the largest city in Orange County, California, asking God if I should leave the pastoral ministry to build a company.

'But Lord,' I said, as needles of doubt pricked my conscience, 'I have been taught all my life that the love of money is the root of *all* evil. How can it then be right that I leave my congregation and devote all my time and energy in the business world?'

Here I was, pacing around the office of my part-time business, contemplating going against the very thing that I had preached many times. I could even then picture the first time I had stood before a packed church and used as my text, Matthew 19:23–24:—'Verily I say unto you . . . it is easier for a camel to go through the eye of a needle, than for a rich man to enter into the kingdom of God.'

I recalled the hush in the congregation at that little wooden church in Idaho Falls, as I insisted, 'Friends, we are on this earth to serve the Lord and to lay up for ourselves treasures in heaven . . . not here on this earth. I know that you've seen those people with their big cars and fancy homes who are so wrapped up in their selfish ambitions that eternal values are far from their minds. It seems to me that their whole purpose in life is to acquire more and more wealth and . . .' pausing for a moment to give real effect to my concluding comments, I added, *they don't care who they step on!'*

Even as a child in the lush Skagit Valley, located in north-west Washington, about sixty miles north of Seattle, and eighty miles south of Vancouver, Canada, I had been taught to believe that wealth and spirituality were completely incompatible.

Now all these years later, my whole life was in a turmoil. I felt that my Christian friends would not understand what I was contemplating doing. Yet, somehow, in the depths of my heart, I knew that God was saying to me, *'I want to make you wealthy beyond your wildest dreams, so you can give it back to me! I want you to forget all your previous concepts and walk through this new experience so others can learn the truth about the biblical concepts of stewardship.'*

For years, along with my wife Carole and our four sons, Don, Dave, Dan and Doug, we had known what it was to sacrifice. We had worn hand-me-down clothes out of the missionary barrel, eaten meat just once a month because we couldn't afford it more often, and taken our 'special offer' coupons to the supermarkets.

To us, however, these inconveniences were no big deal. We had been taught as Christians that to be frugal was a virtue.

Now here I was, possibly on the threshold of great financial success, and I was feeling overwhelmed with guilt. That partly stemmed from the fact that it meant

I would have to resign from my church. And who had ever heard of a pastor leaving the ministry to go into big business? It was usually the other way around.

Yet even as I wrestled with this predicament, I again felt that still small voice I had come to recognize as God's saying, *'Duane, do it for me. The two greatest needs in the Christian world are people and money. I want to use you to be a channel to fund my work; I want to prove myself to you and through you. I'm counting on you!'*

*     *     *

I could see from Carole's face that she was about to explode. I was dog-tired and had been for months. As was my practice, I fell onto the sofa and, almost immediately, felt my eyes go out of focus as I drifted off to sleep. It was six o'clock in the evening.

After what must have been thirty minutes, I felt her hand shaking me.

'Duane, do you feel like eating?' Although Carole's tone was soft, I sensed an undercurrent of anger there too. It was as if she was really asking, 'Why do your outside business affairs mean so much to you? Why can't you just pastor the church and leave it at that?'

I managed to drag myself to the table and began politely nibbling on the roast beef dinner that she had prepared for me. But after a few mouthfuls I couldn't eat any more.

'Do you mind if I go to bed? I've had a hard day.'

That was the trigger for Carole to bring to the surface something she had been trying to hold down for weeks now.

'Duane, there *has* to be an end to this.' She rose to her feet, trembling slightly. 'There has to be some solution. Your business is not only affecting your life, but also the life of the church, and our lives and the children's. This whole situation has become a nightmare for me.'

The words poured from her lips uncontrollably. I felt like I'd been hit by a Sherman tank.

'Let's sleep on it, darling, and talk about it tomorrow.' I just wanted to go to bed. I was too dog tired to fight.

But Carole wouldn't give in that easily.

'Look Duane,' she said, her face by now etched with pain, 'something's got to be settled soon. If it isn't, I'm going to have a breakdown. Do you want me back in the hospital again?'

I looked at my wife. Her face had become as white as milk. Her eyes were pale, like watery diamonds. She was suddenly terribly fragile. And terribly beautiful. I knew that being the wife of an ambitious pastor and the mother of four active sons had taken a big toll on her health. She had been in and out of the hospital on several occasions for a succession of illnesses.

I recalled the time recently when her doctor had called me into his office and warned me Carole was 'a highly emotional woman', and that the 'stress factor in her life, because of your business interests and your work as a pastor, has made life almost impossible for her'.

The white-coated doctor had drummed his finger tips on his desk, then pushed his glasses to the end of his nose and fixed his gaze on me.

'Mr Logsdon,' he had said with a brutal directness, 'you have some big decisions to make, and if you make the wrong ones you could push your wife right over the edge.'

I had walked outside and shielded my eyes against

the bright California sun. I was confused. I brooded on his comments to me. What decision should I make? It seemed to me that I couldn't win whichever way I turned.

# CHAPTER TWO

# North to Alaska

As the front door slammed shut, I felt a wave of excitement sweep over me.

'Bye Mum,' I muttered, running my shaking fingers through a mop of unruly brown hair. 'Take your time at the shops.' This was my big opportunity to repair the wringer of her old washing machine.

I had waited for this moment for several weeks now. I was convinced that I could do it: but whether I could complete it before she returned was another thing.

I hurried quickly to the shed where my dad kept his toolbox. Excitedly I picked it up and hauled it back to my mother's pride and joy—her old washing machine.

I had watched her struggling with the well-used machine and heard the strange sounds that came from the inner depths of the gearbox on the wringer. I knew that Mum could not afford to have it mended, but I also realized that she would never trust me to take it apart and put it back together again. I resolved that as soon as she was out of the house long enough, I would try to fix it.

The risks were high. Failure, I knew, would result in a 'trip to the woodshed' with my dad, so I had to work fast. My hand quivered nervously as I disassembled the shroud, then the rollers. Soon I was opening up the gear case and was removing the greasy gears. Immediately I could see the problem. The bushings on the shaft had to be replaced. I had studied a similar case in *Popular Mechanics* and had filed the application away in my thirteen-year-old brain.

Gently I removed the bushings, and then went back to the toolshed and found a piece of brass pipe. Soon I had drilled out the centre to the same size as the shaft. Now came the moment of truth. Would it fit? I knew that Mum would be back within an hour, so I ran back to the machine. Glory be! It did fit. A hot triumphant joy coursed through me. I quickly reassembled the machine and turned it on. It worked perfectly. Just as I got the final pieces together again I heard heavy footsteps approach, a key turn in the lock and the front door creak open. 'I'm home, son,' called Mum. 'I need a hand with the grocery bags.'

Proud as Punch, I went running towards her, but decided not to tell her about my brilliant piece of renovation straight away. When the last grocery bag was emptied and the last tomato had been stored in the fridge, I turned to her and said, 'Mum, I've got a surprise for you.'

My patient mother had got used to my springing surprises on her, such as getting oil all over my clothes or tearing my trouser leg in my bike chain. 'What is it this time?' she asked. 'Oh, Mum,' I said in mocked frustration, 'It's something nice. *I've fixed your wringer!*'

'You mean that you have taken that apart too? Last week it was the lawn mower, then the carburettor on the oil stove. Where will it all end?'

I reached over and affectionately put my arm around her shoulders and said, 'But Mum, I did it for *you*.' I waited for her beam of delight as she examined the wringer.

Suddenly she responded, 'What's all this grease doing on the rollers then?' I could see frustration written all over her face.

'If I had put some clothes through these messy rollers,' she sighed dropping into a chair, 'we would have had to buy all new clothes and that would have cost a fortune!'

Although this was not the surprise I had intended, I wasn't going to let this interfere with my inner compulsion to discover how just about everything mechanical or electrical worked.

The following year I began my high school education at Mount Vernon High School, a red-brick institution with the look of a castle. To my delight, the school provided a manual training shop. Immediately I found myself absorbed in mechanical drawing and woodwork.

I started off making a three-cornered what-not shelf, and progressed to end tables, then more sophisticated furniture like inlaid coffee table tops, desks, cedar chests, and finally my pride and joy, a walnut desk.

One day, as I stood admiring my handiwork, I was joined by Mr Peterson, the woodwork instructor. 'Duane,' he said, a beam of pride lighting up his face, 'that's a mighty fine piece of work. How would you like to share some of your skills with the first-year students? I want you to teach the basics of woodwork to them.' How could I refuse?

*   *   *

However, life in Mount Vernon (named in 1877 after George Washington's homesite of Mount Vernon, Virginia) was not exactly paradise for me. As in most small towns, there was not too much going on for teenagers. Sure, I could earn a few extra dollars helping my father in my spare time with his plumbing business. But there was no excitement in doing that, so when I heard of the opportunity of going to Alaska for the summer of 1944 to earn some 'big money' I jumped at it.

'Duane,' a friend of mine from school had told me in a confidential manner, 'my uncle runs a cannery on Afognak Island right off the tip of Kodiak, Alaska.

'It's kind of bleak there, Duane,' he had continued, his freckled face lighting up, 'but you could make a potful of money in a short time.'

The whole adventure sounded attractive to me, but I knew there could be a problem. I was only fifteen, and the minimum age for the job was eighteen. I shared this difficulty with my friend.

'Any chance of your "aging" a little?' he chuckled in response. 'After all, you are shaving now. No one will know.'

I rushed home from school to put the plan to my dad. He listened patiently to what I told him about being able to make a large amount of money for working twelve hours on, twelve hours off, for seven days a week in the Alaska cannery.

Dad thoughtfully rubbed his four-o'-clock shadow and posed the question, 'Do you really think you can handle something as tough as that, son? After all, you're still only a kid!'

I was annoyed. 'Of course I could,' I snapped back impatiently. 'And I'm not "only a kid". Kids don't shave. I do!'

So with the tacit approval of my father, I went to Seattle to fill out the application form at the cannery's waterfront office.

The clerk there peered quizzically at me through thick-lens glasses that dwarfed his face and magnified his eyes, and observed, 'You don't look eighteen to me.'

'But I am, sir. Honest I am!' I mustered a smile with the hope I would be convincing.

'Well, if you can get your father to endorse this application and get it back to me in a week, I'll accept you for the summer.'

Amazingly, my father agreed to sign the document. As he handed it back to me, he said, 'Duane, this is not going to be easy but I reckon it will sure be good for you. You'll grow into a man pretty quickly.'

I didn't quite understand what he was saying then. All I could see ahead was adventure and excitement. I thought my heart would pop right out of my chest as I boarded the eighty-two-foot fishing boat that was to take me and a dozen other 'men' to this remote area of Alaska. I was so excited. I had never in my life met folk like the seven hardened, rough and tough fishermen who were crewing the boat.

All of them were tanned and weather-beaten by the sun and salt water. And they all swore, yelled and cursed, yet they all seemed to really understand the sea and did a fine job in getting us the 3,000 miles north to our final destination, one of the remotest areas of the untapped North.

All the thrill I was feeling was abruptly swept away in one day when a terrifying storm suddenly attacked us and caused our boat to bob around in the angry ocean like a little cork. The crew lashed just about everything to the deck or to the bulkheads, while the storm got worse and worse.

I was constantly sick and eventually found myself heaving up . . . nothing! My stomach was churning with fear. I didn't want to die so young!

'Come on son, I'll tie you into your bunk,' offered

Per, a blond Norwegian crewman who had taken pity on me. 'Otherwise, you're going to get smashed against the side and then you'll never be able to make any money!'

I lay there tied down like a pig waiting to be slaughtered. Everything blurred around that one preoccupation—staying alive. I began to ponder what Dad had said to me before I left. But how could an experience like this be 'good' for me?

Almost as quickly as the storm had come up, it disappeared to haunt someone else. I was eventually untied and allowed on deck with the others. I almost wept with relief when I saw land ahead. As we sailed closer, I could see beautiful fir trees clustered together on rocky hills. Then I saw the little wooden dock where we were to land, and the clearing where the cannery was located.

A knot of people stood there to welcome us. Most of the men were unshaven and looked as if they were experiencing a nightmare. But surely, they couldn't have been through anything worse than I had just experienced at sea?

I was shown to my rough quarters in a back room and soon I joined a group of men all working twelve-hour shifts, during which we had to work non-stop filling huge bags with dried fish meal. The meal was to be used for soap and perfume. In an appalling corrugated iron hut, we filled sack after sack to their full weight of 125 pounds.

When the steamships came in, we would also be expected to do our normal shifts and then work dockside unloading them. Often we would be working nearly twenty-four hours a day. After a short time I found my mind whirling with confusion; my whole body ached and was near to a total collapse. Yet the others seemed to take this pressure as a matter of course.

After three weeks, I was close to what I thought was complete mental and physical breakdown. Black despair pressed behind my eyes and my head was constantly thudding. The whole thing had turned into a nightmare. So one of the men, 'Little Olaf', another husky Norwegian, took me in a speedboat from Iron Creek, where the cannery was located, to Kodiak Island, where there was an American doctor.

I was hungry, wretched and miserable, as I shivered in the back of the boat. I began to think of Mount Vernon. It may have been a boring place, but there at least I didn't have to suffer like this. Boy, if only I could be back with my friends at school. That would be heaven.

The bearded doctor gave me a full examination and then asked me to sit down opposite him in his Spartan office.

'Young man, there's nothing physically wrong with you,' he said, shifting in his chair impatiently. 'It appears to me that you've got a good dose of homesickness. You are facing one of the biggest decisions you will probably ever face. You can go home a defeated young man, or you can stick it out and prepare yourself to be a man.'

Confused and taken aback, I could see there was really no way out, so I agreed to try and stick it out until my three months were up.

*   *   *

Part of the process of becoming a man was being exposed to an environment of red-eyed men spending their spare time drinking Scotch whisky and gambling away their money.

Some nights I would sit in the bunkhouse and watch with mouth agape as whisky-fired men would blow their entire week's pay cheque in one evening. The air would be charged like the atmosphere of an electrical storm. As their cash disappeared, they would take a final swig from their Johnnie Walker bottle and then weave their way towards their bunk beds. Some nights there would be about $2,000 in a pot on the table. Their lives seemed to revolve around work, booze and gambling. It all seemed so pointless to me. But then, what did I know about life?

The only other residents on our remote island were Aleuts, natives of that part of the Alaska peninsula. The Aleut girls were particularly beautiful. Their lightly bronzed complexions and oriental eyes made them almost irresistible to the men. And the girls saw the men as a possible way of leaving their sparse surroundings for the excitement of other lands, including the mainland United States.

'Look, kid, keep away from the Aleut broads,' warned Peter, one of the American workers. 'They get friendly with you, then get pregnant by one of their own and blame you. That means you have to marry the girl.'

When the Aleuts had special festivals, many of the men from the cannery would be invited to join in the fun. I went along one day to their village. I sat on my wooden stool, petrified that one of the girls would sidle up to me and try to become friendly.

Peter saw my expression. 'Say, kid, see that one over there? Well, she's got her eye on you. Be careful, or she'll trap you.'

The girl was certainly beautiful, and she carried that beauty without self-consciousness, with an easy, erect confidence. Each time she tried to catch my eye I turned my face away, but couldn't stop it flushing blood red.

I tried to swallow but my mouth was too dry. I felt awkward and self-conscious.

One day I saw the same girl purposefully striding up the muddy street towards the cannery. I got so scared that I hid in my bunkhouse until she left.

Surprisingly, the three months did go quickly. It was a very different young man who boarded the boat back to Seattle. Sticking it out gave me a new confidence. I felt that if I could survive this, I could survive anything.

The very clerk that had signed me up in Seattle handed me an envelope containing a staggering $1,000 in notes. By today's standards, that would be worth about $15,000—a real fortune!

'Not bad for an "eighteen-year-old",' he chuckled as I counted it. I knew he *knew*, but neither of us said anything.

I became something of a folk hero back in Mount Vernon. I was able to open a bank account and buy my first car, a 1929 Model-A Ford. I paid $250 for this four-door sedan. I didn't have a driving licence as I wasn't yet sixteen, so again I needed my father's help.

'Look, Dad, anyone who could go to Alaska and make that kind of money, ought to be entitled to a licence. After all, I'm going to be sixteen in two months. Why don't you just sign for me right now and say I'm already sixteen?' Much against his better judgement, he did, and soon I was able to take the test. I passed first time.

So now I was the proud owner of a current account, a four-door sedan, a driver's licence, and a host of new friends. I was now the richest and most popular kid at

Mount Vernon High.

I quickly discovered that money talks.

# CHAPTER THREE

# Popeye

'Duane, I lied for you.' One single tear, very large and silent, ran down Carole Noble's cheek. 'I know I shouldn't have done it, but I can't stop thinking about you.'

My mouth twitched and my eyes filled with puzzlement.

'But I thought your dad didn't mind your coming to the prom with me?'

She smiled nervously and reached over to touch the back of my hand.

'He has forbidden me ever to go out with you. He saw you in a bar and feels you are not good enough for me.' Her cheeks and eyelids turned bright crimson.

'To be honest, I don't think he feels any boy is good enough for me. I guess that's the price you pay when you are an only child.'

I heard that her dad, Rusty Noble, had seen me in the Garden Gate Tavern. It was on the other side of town and I had slipped in there with a few school pals, who, as usual, expected me to pick up the tab for the beers we consumed. Maybe we were a little loud and obnoxious, but this was an evening of celebration for all of us. For, finally, my thousand dollars had run out, and I had announced that this had to be our last fling at my personal expense. I could see by their looks that I was about to lose many of my 'friends', but still there would be others.

In fact, just after I became completely insolvent, I had become aware of Carole, a dark-haired, shyly pretty girl, who didn't seem to mind that I was now broke. I was what we called the 'Yell King' for the Bulldogs Football Team at Mount Vernon Union High School, and Carole was one of my cheer leaders. I liked her so much I had asked her to be my date for the prom, which was the school's social event of the year.

The effect of that night at the prom triggered something inside me. Suddenly this charming girl, whom I had been taking for granted, took hold of my thoughts and I realized I wanted to spend the rest of my life with her. But up to this time, all I seemed to have done was to tell her the intimate secrets of my other dates. It was beginning to dawn on me how painful that must have been for her.

'Yes, Carole Noble's going to be my steady,' I had vowed to myself.

But then had come the blazing row between Carole and her stern father.

'No daughter of mine is going to go out with a boozer,' he had thundered. 'He's just a kid playing at being a man.' The anger in his voice was unmistakable.

'But, Dad, you must have been drinking, too, if you saw him in the tavern.'

His face became red with rage.

Carole realized that there could be no further argument. There had been many previous disagreements over boys, and Carole realized the only way to overcome this situation was to lie.

So she told her father that she was going to spend the night at a friend's house. That part was true, but she neglected to add that she would also be dancing with me at the prom.

I turned the key in the ignition of my dad's 1946 Chevy Sedan, which he had lent me for this important evening, and listened to the engine whine.

I stepped on the throttle, turned the radio up louder, and said, 'Okay Carole, let's forget about these problems and have a good time tonight. We can work them out later.'

We did! Although Mr Noble never did quite approve of me, he finally allowed me to have his daughter's hand in marriage. And on August 26th, 1949, he gave Carole away at our wedding at the First Baptist Church of Mount Vernon.

Carole looked radiant in her white flowing gown, which had come as a gift from her grandfather, a farmer from Missouri.

He had told his granddaughter, 'Honey, I'm going to sell my prized dapple-grey work horses to buy you your wedding dress.'

I felt my knees become weak and my hands tremble as she pledged to take me as her husband 'in sickness and in health . . . for better for worse . . . till death us do part.'

Soon I had placed the gold ring on the third finger of her left hand and we had kissed. Mrs Carole Logsdon was now linked with me for life.

*    *    *

'Yes, young man, what can I do for you?' Bud Cannon held out his hand and gave me a warm, friendly smile that assured me he had had years of experience in selling houses.

'Er, well, I'll be honest, sir, I need a house for my

wife and myself. We've just been married and . . . well, we plan to start a family.'

I explained that we were temporarily staying in a tiny one-bedroomed apartment, but that really would not be adequate for us if a child should come along.

'How much money do you have for a deposit? You realize that you must put something down?'

I nodded. 'Well sir, I don't actually have a cent. But I do own a 1941 five-passenger Chevrolet coupé. I am sure I could sell it for $500. It is a real sharp car and $500 would be a bargain. I would be willing to part with it and walk everywhere if it meant that I could get into a house of our own.'

Cannon must have considered me a good risk. Within four days, he had made an appointment to show us a two-bedroom bungalow right opposite the red brick church where we had been married.

'I like your style, Duane. I think this is a great opportunity for you to get started in your own home. I've even got someone to finance a second mortgage for you. What do you think about that?'

Carole wasn't so sure if this was to be the house of her dreams or not. Especially as she had discovered that a bank of earth had collapsed in a rain storm and was stacked up against the back of the house.

'Don't worry about that, Carole. Duane looks in good shape. He could soon fix that up and make this place really nice.

'So what do you say? Do you want it?'

She nodded. And soon we had moved in and, with the help of friends, removed the bank of earth.

*     *     *

'Duane, it's time to go to the hospital.'

I started up into a sitting position and clawed my way back to a waking reality. I sleepily squinted at the clock on our bedside table.

'But it's only five in the morning!' I said in a sleep-blurred voice.

The waves of pain kept coming and Carole cried out.

'Okay, we'll go, but let me shave first. You know I hate appearing in public with stubble on my face.'

Carole could hardly speak. Both the pain and my insistence on shaving had taken her voice away.

I decided that a taxi was the only way we could make it in time to the hospital, so I called the nearest company.

'Hey, would you send a taxi over here immediately. My wife's having a baby.'

I slammed down the receiver. 'They'll be right over, Carole. Don't worry, everything will be fine.'

Carole looked at me.

'Oh Duane, they won't be right over. You forgot to tell them our address!'

When we eventually arrived at the white-walled hospital, I dashed round to her side of the taxi, opened the door and helped to ease her out. Then I grabbed her hand and marched her towards the entrance. It wasn't until we had registered that I realized she had been carrying her own suitcase.

I paced up and down as the minutes ticked by. Two hours later I couldn't stand the tension any longer. I tip-toed towards the delivery room and, after making sure no one was watching, I put my right eye to the keyhole.

I could see that Carole was in the final moments of labour. The door suddenly flew open and I fell backwards, clasping my eye.

'Oh, no, I've been blinded,' I screamed. 'I'll never see again. . . .'

The nurse who had been responsible for this 'accident' had no sympathy at all.

'Anyone who peeks through keyholes deserves no sympathy,' she said. 'Now go and sit down and we'll let you know the news when we have it.'

Ten minutes later I heard a cry from inside the delivery room and then the nurse came out. She allowed herself the luxury of a thin smile, and then said 'Mr Logsdon, you are the father of a beautiful baby boy. He weighs 7lb 2 oz.'

She peered closely at my eye that was beginning to swell up, and added, 'I hope when he grows up he doesn't start looking through keyholes like his father. That can be a dangerous habit.'

# CHAPTER FOUR

# *The Fool on the Hill*

I leaned heavily on the rake and watched. From our front garden we could see a steady stream of well-dressed people heading up the steep hill and into the large church where we had been married. We were settled in our new home on the hill and had planted a lawn.

Carole came outside with our struggling son Don ensconced in his baby-walker.

'What a bunch of fools,' I remarked to Carole as I watched the late stragglers hurrying into the sanctuary.

'Imagine wasting the only good weather we have had for weeks by going inside that stuffy old church!' I watched Don stretch his legs and gurgle with delight. Then I turned to Carole.

'Hey, that was a great time at the dance last night. I really had a ball!'

She paused for a moment, biting her lower lip. Then she responded, 'You sure did! You danced half the night with Bill's wife.'

I wasn't going to take that. 'You can talk!' I snapped back. 'It seems to me that you didn't do too badly yourself. I saw you jiving with Dave for over an hour.'

It seemed that every Sunday morning turned into an argument over the good or bad times we had had the previous night, and who our dancing partner happened to be.

Still, those Saturday nights were a diversion from the boredom of being a fuel delivery driver in a small town. The hours I worked were long and mostly uninteresting. I would come home at night feeling tired and frustrated.

We both began to feel cheated. We had expected a romantic, wonderful relationship, but now after less than two years of marriage we were not experiencing what we had hoped—something was missing, even though we knew we loved each other.

One day, during a time of deep depression for both of us, I sat down with Carole and began to share with her how I felt.

'There must be more to life than this,' I said. She nodded, but said nothing.

I headed for our bedroom and flopped on the bed. For a time I stared aimlessly at the ceiling, and then my left hand dropped down at the side of the bed. It touched a book that lay on the bedside table and I looked to see what it was.

It turned out to be a copy of the Bible that had lain unopened since we were married. I picked it up and propped myself against the pillow. Blowing the dust off the cover, I flipped the pages until I came to Matthew 7:24–27. There I began reading the words of Jesus where he said, 'Therefore whosoever heareth these sayings of mine, and doeth them, I will liken him unto a wise man, which built his house upon a rock: and the rain descended, and the floods came, and the winds blew, and beat upon that house; and it fell not: for it was founded upon a rock. And every one that heareth these sayings of mine, and doeth them not, shall be likened unto a foolish man, which built his house upon the sand: and the rain descended, and the floods came, and the winds blew, and beat upon that house; and it fell; and great was the fall of it.'

As I closed the Bible, I began to realize that I was just like the foolish man who had built his house on the sand. I had no foundation to my life at all. Something vital was missing.

*     *     *

Maud Hansen's voice rose stridently, 'You know, my dear, if you are not a believer, you won't go up to meet the Lord at the rapture of the church.'

I stopped at the front door, intrigued to hear more.

'Yes, Carole, in the last days rocks will fall on people and blood will flow deep and red in the streets.'

My wife was deeply affected by the comments of this elderly neighbour who liked to encase herself in black. Even though she was kind and sincere I thought her to be a religious nut.

I walked into the kitchen to find Carole obviously distressed by her comments.

'Hello, Mrs Hansen,' I hissed disapprovingly as I held out my hand to her. 'I was just telling your wife how wonderful it is to be prepared to meet the Lord when he comes,' was her response.

I groaned, wondering what in the world we were in for. I didn't want her fire-and-brimstone preaching here.

'Duane,' she said, her kind eyes making me feel uncomfortable, 'God has a plan for your life. Are you ready to accept it? It is the most wonderful thing that can happen to a person.'

I coughed and said nothing.

'Well, if you want to know more about this, why not go across the street on Sunday to the church? You'll learn about Jesus there. I would invite you to my church, but there are no young people around your age there. Anyway, I would be happy to stay with your little boy while you went to your church.'

Feeling trapped, I reluctantly agreed to go. Next Sunday morning she came in ten minutes before the start of the service. I had put on a suit, and Carole looked great in her new dress.

The usher seated us in the centre of the middle section of the sanctuary. There were ten people on either side of us. I know—I counted them. I nearly broke into laughter as the guest preacher came onto the platform.

'He looks as if he is about to conduct a funeral service,' I whispered to Carole, as we eyed him in his black suit and tie, firmly clasping a huge black Bible.

Although Mrs Hansen's approach turned us both off, we were strangely ready to be convinced that there could be a better way.

At the start of his sermon, the bushy-eyed orator produced a copy of *Reader's Digest* and began quoting humorous items from it. Then he shared a few jokes. He seemed to be bending over backwards not to offend. Not once did he quote from his Bible.

Half-way through the glib sermon, I felt a wave of disgust sweep over me. 'This guy is nothing but a performer; he is trying to impress the people,' I observed sardonically to my embarrassed wife.

'Well, he doesn't impress me! Let's go. There is nothing here for us.' I was bitterly disappointed.

Carole's face turned crimson as we inched our way to the right, past the ten people, and then into the aisle. As we made our way out into the street, I said, so all could hear, 'I guess the answer doesn't lie in religion.'

Mrs Hansen was surprised to see us back so early. 'It

was terrible,' I told her. 'The preacher didn't answer any of my questions. There was nothing there for my heart. The whole thing was a charade. It seemed to me that all the people there were playing a game called "church".' Mrs Hansen put down the Bible she was reading.

'My dears, would you try another church? I know one that has a lot of young married couples like you.'

I wasn't quite sure how to respond to this situation.

'Please go,' she continued. 'You might find what you are looking for there.'

'I doubt it, Mrs Hansen, but I will give it one more try.'

*     *     *

I squeezed Carole's hand as the singing began at the Emmanuel Baptist Church, a white stucco building on the corner of Cleveland and Hazel Street.

'Hey, this seems more like it,' I told Carole, as she mouthed the words of a chorus that she didn't really know.

'Just sing, darling, sing,' was her reply.

After the preliminaries, the pastor, Thurlow Yazley, a tall strikingly good-looking man, began his sermon. A few minutes into the message I began to feel that someone had briefed him on my story. It seemed that everything that he was saying had my name attached to it.

'The way of the transgressor is hard,' he said quoting from Proverbs, as I sat there transfixed. 'It is hard, it is harder, it is the hardest,' he added.

'There is a way that seems right to a man, but the end thereof are the ways of death.'

He was pointing out from Scripture that I was on a

road to destruction.

At the close of the sermon I was totally convinced. Pastor Yaxley gave an invitation for those who wished to accept Christ.

All were standing at this time and he suggested that those who wanted to make this commitment should raise their hands. I wanted prayer, but I didn't want anyone else to know, especially my wife, who was on my left side. So I gingerly raised my right hand.

I didn't know she felt the same, and that she raised her left hand at the very same moment.

The pastor pleaded with the people who had responded to come forward and accept Jesus Christ. That was expecting too much, I thought. I didn't move. Nor did Carole.

Soon he had made his way to the back of the church to shake hands with the congregation. As we tried to slip past, he stepped forward, extending a warm handshake. 'Is there any way that I can help you make a decision today?' I was embarrassed. This seemed like such a private matter and I was angry. 'When I want your help,' I snapped abrasively, 'I'll call you!'

As we both walked out, neither one of us talking, I recalled that the pastor had announced there was going to be an evangelistic meeting in a nearby town.

I mentioned it to Carole and she agreed to go with me.

'That's the church of the pastor who married us,' she pointed out. 'Let's just go and see what they have to offer there.' Mrs Hansen came over again and we drove the ten miles to the service. We sat there with a spirit of expectancy, and felt the electrifying liveliness of the music.

The young, stocky evangelist began to preach the gospel.

'Ladies and gentlemen, I want to tell you that all have sinned and come short of the glory of God. Christ died for our sins. Your sins.' This was the same thing we had heard from Mrs Hansen and Pastor Yaxley.

He asked for response for prayer by raising of hands.

Again both of us, eyes closed, shot our hands in the air, my right and Carole's left.

'I want those of you who put up your hands to come to the front,' he requested.

Neither of us moved. We were anchored to the pew, feeling both angry and embarrassed.

After the service, the evangelist quickly walked to the door. As we passed him, he smiled and shook my hand. 'And what is your name?'

'Duane,' I snapped, my voice trembling with anger, 'that's my name!'

We drove back to our home in total silence.

The following week was terrible for both of us. There was a war going on inside us, and we would lapse into long silences. I tried to ward off my feeling, but found it impossible. We didn't go to church that next weekend. I remember tossing restlessly in bed each night. I knew what I had to do, but I was afraid of the cost. I feared that I would be ridiculed by all of our partying friends and also by our families, none of whom were Christians. I thought that if my lifestyle changed too drastically I might also lose my job because no one there was a believer and they might not want a 'religious fanatic' to work with.

The following week, on a Monday morning— February 18th, 1952—I had reached a point of decision. I drove by lorry to my home on that freezing day to have lunch with Carole. As I pulled on my heavy overcoat and started to leave, I told her, 'I am going to go to the church south of town and talk to that preacher.'

I got into the lorry as she stood there speechless. I drove the three-quarters of a mile to the front of the parsonage and parked. I felt incredibly nervous. Ice cracked underfoot as I somehow made my way up the five steps of the front porch supported by two white pillars and knocked on the door. The wind made me tighten the woollen scarf around my neck.

There was no reply. All of a sudden I felt abandoned. I turned around and went back to the lorry. I had a couple of deliveries to make a short distance south. I decided that on my way back I would turn off to the church. It was 3.00 p.m. when I parked my lorry and walked to the door. This time Pastor Yaxley answered my knock.

'Yes, sir, may I help you?'

Before he could say any more, I responded, my breath steaming in the freezing air, 'Pastor, I've got an awful burden. May I come in?'

# CHAPTER FIVE

# *A New Mummy and Daddy*

Thurlow Yaxley looked more like an American grid-iron football player than a pastor. He was tall and thick-set, yet his angular face gave the impression of a man with love for his fellow human beings.

As I sat opposite him in his simple study, I knew that here was a man I could trust completely. Integrity was etched into every line of his face.

But I soon discovered that Pastor Yaxley didn't want me to trust in *him*, but in the Bible.

'Duane,' he said softly, 'I'm going to open the Scriptures and read a few verses to you.'

I was puzzled. 'Look, Pastor, there's no need for that, I'm already convinced. I need to get rid of this burden.'

He smiled gently. 'Yes, but you must completely understand what you are going to do. I want God's word to sink deep into your heart.'

With that he ruffled the pages of his well-used Bible with his large hands and stopped when he came to the epistle to the Romans. He read to me verse 10 of chapter 3, 'There is none righteous, no, not one.' He then moved on to the 23rd verse: 'For all have sinned, and come short of the glory of God.'

Next he turned to Romans, chapter 5, verses 10 and 11. In a soft voice that belied his king-sized frame, he read, 'For if, when we were enemies, we were recon-

ciled to God by the death of his Son, much more, being reconciled, we shall be saved by his life. And not
only so, but we also joy in God through our Lord Jesus
Christ, by whom we have now received the atone-
ment.'

Pastor Yaxley turned and locked his eyes tight on
mine. 'Duane, you can see there that none of us are
righteous or deserve salvation. That means that we are
all doomed to an eternity without God. There is no
hope for any of us, even a pastor!'

He could read the confusion in my eyes.

'Well, there is no hope . . . without Jesus!' His jaw
tightened for a moment, then he quickly turned to
John, chapter 3, verse 16. 'Duane, this verse is, truly
the gospel in a nutshell. I want you to take it and read
it out loud so you can fully understand it.'

My hands trembled slightly as I picked up his Bible
and began reading that momentous verse: 'For God so
loved the world, that he gave his only begotten Son,
that whosoever believeth in him should not perish, but
have everlasting life.'

It was then that I really understood what salvation
was all about. None of us could save ourselves from
the dues of our sin, so God sent Jesus, his Son, to pay
the penalty for us on the cross.

'That's incredible, Pastor. You know, I have an only
son, Don, and I don't think I could let someone kill
him for whatever reason.'

'But God loved us so much that he allowed evil men
to kill his Son so as to redeem his own creation.'

I was speechless for a moment. Then Pastor Yaxley
leaned over to me and said, 'Duane, wouldn't you now
like to kneel and ask Jesus Christ into your life?'

Feeling numb, I responded immediately. 'Yes, I
would.'

The pastor sank to the carpeted floor beside his chair. I followed his lead.

'Right, Duane, I am going to say a prayer and I want you to repeat it after me. Will you do that?'

Again I nodded my head.

'Lord, I know that I'm a sinner and I can't save myself. . . .' In a voice that was no more than a whisper I repeated the prayer.

'. . . I believe that Jesus Christ died on the cross to save me from my sins. In the best way I know, I now accept him as my personal Saviour from sin. In Jesus' name. Amen.'

It seemed too simple. I stood up feeling strangely disappointed. I had somehow expected to hear angels sing and bells ring.

But all was quiet.

The Pastor extended his huge hand to me. 'Welcome to the kingdom,' he said brightly. Then he saw the look of disappointment on my face.

'What's the problem, Duane? Is it that you feel something more dramatic should have happened?'

'I guess that's it. I don't really feel any different, I'm not sure that I have been saved.'

Pastor Yaxley's eyes were soft with understanding. 'That's not an unusual feeling, Duane. The problem is that you are depending on how you feel, rather than in a faith that God will do what he has promised to do.

'I want to ask you a sincere question. Did you truly mean what you just prayed?'

'Yes, sir, I really did.'

'Okay, on the basis of your sincere prayer, let's look again at God's word to see what you have just done.'

Pastor Yaxley turned first to the first epistle of John, chapter 5, verses 10 and 11. 'Now read those verses, Duane.'

I cleared my throat and began: 'He that believeth on the Son of God hath the witness in himself: he that believeth not God hath made him a liar; because he believeth not the record that God gave of his Son. And this is the record, that God hath given to us eternal life, and this life is in his Son.'

The pastor came over and put his arm on my shoulder.

'Duane, on the basis of that reading, do you *have* Jesus Christ the Son of God in your heart?'

I said I thought so, but I still wasn't completely sure.

'Read it again,' he said.

I did and again he asked, 'Duane, did you ask Jesus Christ into your life?'

'Yes,' I said more confidently this time.

'If so,' he continued, 'do you have the Son?'

Suddenly the Scriptures became clear to me. 'Well, based on God's promise there in those verses, I do have God's Son, Jesus. Yes, I suppose I do!'

All of a sudden, I felt a deep warmth flood my body.

At last I had the assurance that I had simply done what God said I needed to do for the forgiveness of my sins. I had invited Jesus Christ into my heart and *he had come in*! That sense of guilt that had wrapped itself around me like a chain had finally been snapped and I was free!

I bowed my head and began thanking him. It was from the depths of my heart.

'Oh, God,' I almost shouted, 'thank you for allowing me to become one of your children. Thank you for forgiving me for my sins and . . . well, giving me new life. Whatever you want me to do, wherever you want me to go, I'll do it . . .' I promised.

The pastor came over to me and gave me a bone-crushing bear hug.

'Has the burden gone?' he asked, his face beaming.

I nodded. 'It sure has. It sure has.'

Then he asked me about Carole. 'Is she a Christian?'

In the drama of the moment, I had forgotten all about my wife. 'No, sir,' I admitted, 'she's not a Christian yet.'

He scratched his chin.

'Oh would it be all right if my wife and I called at your home tonight? Maybe we could share the Good News with her too.'

I knew Carole would be hopping mad if I arranged for this couple to come around to 'convert' her. But what could I do?

I found a nearby call box and phoned Carole.

'Carole, would you mind if Pastor Yaxley and his wife came over for a few minutes tonight?'

'But why?' she was perplexed.

'Well, you see, I've just left the pastor's study, where I became a Christian.'

'You what?' There was a silence for a few moments, as she tried to digest what I had just told her. Then I repeated my news. 'Look, honey, they are going to come at about 7.30 p.m. Could you get yourself ready?'

She let out a palpable gasp, then there was a long pause at the end of the line.

'Duane,' Carole responded, a slight insinuation of sarcasm in her voice, 'if you are serious about becoming a Christian, there's another job I'm going to have to do first before they arrive.'

'What's that?'

'Clear away all your empty beer bottles from under the sink!'

*       *       *

As I had predicted, Carole was livid with me when I got home.

'Duane, how could you put me in such an embarrassing situation?' The anger in her voice was unmistakable.

I tried to calm her down, but she wouldn't have it.

'Duane, I'll never forgive you for this!'

Just then the front door bell rang. I dashed to the door, feeling that if Carole opened it she might say something that we would all later regret.

Pastor and Mrs Yaxley came in and both began unbuttoning their coats. I took them and before I could stop her, Grace Yaxley went over to a disconsolate Carole and slipped an arm around her shoulder.

'Isn't it wonderful dear, what happened to Duane today? Wouldn't you like to make your home a truly Christian home?'

I waited for the explosion.

I turned and looked at my wife. Tears suddenly appeared in her eyes and a flush spread across her cheeks. 'Yes, I would! I really would!' I thought I was hearing things, but I wasn't. Carole had meant it sincerely.

The four of us knelt together on the carpet of our lounge, and, just as I had done, Carole invited Jesus Christ into her life. It was a moment of ecstasy that neither of us will ever forget.

At last, we were united in the love of Christ.

After much happy conversation, fuelled by coffee, the pastor and his wife left and Carole and I walked hand-in-hand to our bedroom. It was then we noticed our fast-growing son, Don, was standing up in his cot. He had been watching all that had been going on through the partially open door.

'Hey, little one,' said Carole, choking back the tears

of joy, 'you've got a new Mummy and Daddy.'

'New Mummy, new Daddy,' he repeated.

# CHAPTER SIX

# You Can't Out-give God

Pastor Yaxley looked unusually serious. 'Duane,' he said, 'if you can stay out of the ministry, do. *Stay out!*'

I looked at him in disbelief. I had expected my spiritual leader to be delighted that I was beginning to feel the call of God to be a pastor.

But before I could express my feelings, he went on, his voice edged with steel.

'But if you *can't* get rid of those feelings, then God really has his hand on your life and you should go ahead with theological training.'

Pastor Yaxley explained that if I was to go into the ministry, I needed to have total peace about it.

'It is also important, Duane, that Carole is completely behind you,' he added.

With that counsel, I began really seeking God's will. Should I leave my job delivering fuel oil and face an uncertain future? After all, we had just moved into our new home and I had recently been given a substantial rise in salary. Also, there was such close fellowship with other couples in the church—like Floyd and Dorothy Hagman, Daryl and Marion Countryman, and Joe and Ann Farina—that I was loth to leave them.

I also realized that my delivery rounds gave me an opportunity to witness for Christ. We had a local mission field, at least for the time being.

One of my regular customers, Frank Mingler, an elderly gentleman, came out to me one day as I was filling his central heating oil tank.

'Duane, can I ask you a personal question?' he suddenly asked.

'Sure, Mr Mingler. What is it?'

'You seem so happy these days. What happened?'

'Well,' I answered as I pulled the nozzle-end from his tank, 'I guess the change came about when I accepted Jesus Christ into my life as my Saviour and Lord.'

He swallowed with embarrassment and a moustache of perspiration appeared on his upper lip.

'I guess I walked into that one,' I heard him mutter as he quickly returned to his house.

Little did either of us know, at that moment, that just two days later Mr Mingler would suffer a stroke which would partially paralyse him. When I heard about it, I immediately went to the hospital to see him. I was shocked at the change in his appearance. He lay there, deathly white. I could see he was failing fast and that his life hung by a thread.

I took his hand and leaned over to speak to him.

'Mr Mingler, if God called you into eternity very soon, would you be ready to meet him?'

He looked at me sadly.

Although he couldn't speak clearly I could hear him say, 'No, I wouldn't.'

'Would you like to know this same Jesus who changed my life?'

His face suddenly broke into a smile.

He nodded his head and I could see the sincerity of his response.

I stood by his bedside, my arm around his shoulders, as he weakly but firmly prayed the 'sinner's prayer' with me.

Six hours later he was dead.

Over the next few months, I had led scores of people in our valley to Christ. I was filled with such a zeal to share my faith with others—all, that is, except my parents. I had a real mental block about telling them.

Finally, I felt that I had to talk to them. On a beautiful spring day, as birds chirped and flowers were beginning to bloom, I drove with Carole towards their home in the next town of Sedro Woolley.

I felt an optimism deep down inside that they would be delighted with our news. I suppose I expected them to immediately fall to their knees and follow our example.

It was quite a shock after I had told them the whole story of our conversions, when my father turned to me and said, 'Well, son, if that's what you want, that's fine. But don't force it on us.'

Before I could respond, he added, 'And, one further thing, when you come here in the future, leave your religion on the doorstep. I don't want any of that nonsense in here.'

I looked at my father with deep compassion. I knew his life was empty, yet he couldn't see it.

'Dad, if that's what you want, I won't preach at you or Mum. But you can't stop me doing something else.'

'What's that?' His eyes filled with great puzzlement.

'You won't be able to stop me from praying for you.'

*       *       *

Carole looked bewildered as I dropped a financial bombshell on her.

I was munching a hurried breakfast of cornflakes washed down with orange juice. 'I know I only bring home $59 a week from my job and we've hardly got any furniture in this place, but I feel God is convicting me of something. I really believe that I should be tithing 10 per cent of my money to God's work.'

Before I could go any further with my homily, Carole cut in.

'But Duane, we don't even have coffee in the house, and you are saying we should give away our last dollars.'

I nodded. 'I believe that if Jesus Christ is really our Saviour and we've made him Lord, then we had better get moving on the financial side, and do what I believe the Scripture teaches us—honour him with our income.'

'What income?' she laughed ironically. 'We can hardly live on what you bring in now.' I could see Carole wasn't convinced. I also knew what I was saying did sound lunatic on a human level. Here we were, almost stone broke, and I was suggesting that we give away the little we had left.

'Carole,' I said, looking straight at her, 'I'm not only saying we should be giving our money to God, but that we should also smile about it.'

I picked up my Bible that was lying on the table and turned it to Colossians 3:17, and read aloud, 'And *whatsoever* ye do in word or deed, do all in the name of the Lord Jesus, giving thanks to God and the Father by him.'

Closing the holy book, I continued, 'Let's become cheerful givers. On Sunday I'm going to start by putting my first tithe in the collection plate at church.

'After all,' I added with a confident grin, 'God has promised to supply *all* our needs. In Philippians 4:19 it says, "But my God shall supply all your need according to his riches in glory by Christ Jesus."'

Carole came around the kitchen table to me, her eyes now brimming. 'Look Duane, I really want to believe with you. I want to walk in faith with you, so I'm going to make a pledge with you that in the future we will give God the first 10 per cent of *all* our income. God gets the first 10 per cent not the left-overs. We will somehow have to live off the rest.'

Within hours of making that pledge, I received my first offer of part-time work, and that was shortly followed by many other jobs, which more than doubled my income in weeks.

One day, as I walked through the door after a long but satisfying day, Carole rushed at me and threw her arms around me.

'What's that for?' I asked.

'It's because the Lord has taught me a real lesson, Duane. Since we made that pledge to tithe, God has really begun to bless us financially. I've come to realize that you *can't out-give God. . . .*'

Shortly after this, we faced another crisis. God had really begun to bless us, and we had found a new house that we wanted to move into.

'Duane, it's the nicest place I've ever seen,' said Carole excitedly as we looked around it. 'But I suppose we will need to sell our present place first before we can have this.'

She was right, so I put it up for sale. We soon had our first prospective buyer, a man called Joe Jones who was in his late sixties. As we showed him around the property, his eyes lit up.

'You know, this is just wonderful. I'm getting married soon and this would be great for us.'

We exchanged glances which said he seemed a little old to be getting married. He said he'd think it over and come back again.

Shortly after he left us, we received another knock at the front door. It was an official from the Highway Department. He told us that it looked like a big motorway was to be built close by and this would mean we would lose our house.

'The one next door will probably go too, but you'll be glad to hear that the church across the way will be okay,' he added.

The official said it was almost certain this project would go through and we would be paid a fair price for the house. However, we didn't really want to wait, as we needed the cash now to get our new 'dream home'.

A few days later, the bridegroom-to-be arrived back at our front door. Now we had a real crisis to face. If we told him the news, he would probably not want to buy. If we didn't and then he discovered about the motorway, he would be very angry with us.

'Look, Mr Jones, before we go any further, I must tell you something. . . .'

'Mr Logsdon, I don't care what you tell me, I want this house for the future Mrs Jones and myself. It's really great.'

'But you don't understand.'

I took a deep breath and then told him the whole story. Instead of being angry, his face suddenly blossomed into a confident grin.

'Look, Mr Logsdon, the State of Washington can just as well buy this place from me as they can you. I'll take it.'

Months later, the State bought the site from him, and he was able to move the complete home to a site on the other side of town.

I made a profit of $2,300 from the deal—and of course, 10 per cent of that went to the church. I had quickly discovered you really can't out-give God.

# CHAPTER SEVEN

# The Challenge and the Call

I knew this feeling I had about going into the ministry had to come to a head. Finally it did, one spring afternoon in 1952.

The fir trees glimmered grey-green in the sunshine as I drove my lorry out into the clearing where I so often went to spend time alone with God. Soon I was on my knees.

'Lord,' I cried out to a background of humming crickets in the surrounding long grass, 'if you want me to sell our home and possessions, I'll do it.'

Tears began to well up in my eyes, 'Lord, I don't care where you lead me and Carole, we'll do it.'

This was the point of total commitment for me.

A deep peace entered my soul. I knew that God had a special plan for my life and all I had to do was to follow him—*one step at a time.*

Carole took my news very coolly. She was in a bedroom with Dave, our second son who had been born some eight months before. She looked distraught after another sleepless night and a day of changing nappies. There were dark circles under her eyes.

'Duane, I don't doubt the call you have had and I'll follow you anywhere, but I must warn you that I'm frightened of the consequences.'

Carole did indeed look scared. 'Do you realize that we are going to have to give up this home of ours and go somewhere thousands of miles from here? We'll not see our friends and families for months on end.'

I was speechless. I looked at her, blinking for a moment, trying to take in her meaning.

'And Duane,' she continued, the words tumbling out as if a cork had been pulled, 'if we are called to Africa, I'm sure that I could cope with the snakes.'

I had been so much into my own thoughts that I had not considered for one moment that Carole was suffering anguish about moving out of our present safe life. We had our friends at the church, our Bible study group, and Carole had the boys to care for. She knew each week what income she would have for food and clothing. Now came the possibility of moving outside of that security to a life full of insecurity and change.

One night, Carole went on her own to a rally where Dr Louis Talbot made an altar call for those who wished to receive Christ for the first time, or even to commit their lives fully to the Christian ministry.

She went forward.

'Duane, I can't fully explain what happened,' she told me later that night through a sheen of tears. 'But I came to a point where I realized I was following you just because I was your wife. But I didn't feel any of God's love in it. In fact, I felt that God was being cruel towards me by taking me out of my secure life and pushing me out of the nest into the unknown.

'You know,' she continued, her face hot and burning, 'I love you so much that I've completely submerged my desires just to please you. I really have had deep fears, but I haven't wanted to share them with you because you might feel I am not spiritual.

'But tonight I tried to give all of those fears to God. I know I will still have problems, but I don't want to be crippled inside any more. I do love the Lord and want to serve him.'

I suddenly felt very tender towards Carole; very protective. I hadn't for one moment understood what she had been going through. I reached across and took her hands. It was then that I saw she had some bloody cuts on them.

'Honey, what happened? How did you get those injuries?'

She took out her handkerchief to wipe away the tears.

'Oh,' she said nonchalantly, 'I was crying so much on the way home that I couldn't see properly through the windscreen. The car swerved off the road and finished up in a ditch. But I'm fine now. I managed to back the car out and drive on home.'

I kissed away the last of her tears. 'The time for crying has stopped,' I said gently. 'Let's never stop talking to each other. We've got to be a team in this.'

It wasn't long before I was writing off for catalogues from Bible schools around the United States. They came in from big and small alike. Each time some literature arrived, we would take time to pray over it and ask God to show us which ones I should apply to.

Finally, we both felt I should write to the school furthest from our home—Bob Jones University in Greenville, South Carolina. It seemed to me that it had an appealing mixture of evangelism and zeal, as well as many excellent classes, especially in the fine arts.

After receiving my school records, which were not too flattering, the university said they would accept me only on probation for one year. And that meant I had to be willing to take one term of algebra and English without credit.

'That means you may have to study there for a total

of four-and-a-half years,' said Carole. 'That's an awfully long time. And how will we raise the money to pay for all your fees?'

I told her I wasn't sure.

'All I can say is I feel that if it's to be Bob Jones, God will provide. I just know he will.'

Now came two major problems that could stop my enrolling as a student for the autumn term of 1953. So if the Lord really wanted me there he had to clear the way through both of them.

I took my first difficulty to my boss, John Martin, at the oil supply company where I worked.

'John,' I told him in his cramped office, 'I've got some news for you. I've tentatively enrolled as a student in the School of Religion at Bob Jones University for September. But you could stop my going.'

'How do you mean, Duane?' He was surprised.

'Well, John, you see I promised to give you one month's notice if I ever leave. But now I need to leave almost straight away. If you hold me to that promise, of course I'll stay. But if you let me go, I'll just about make it in time.'

John thought for a moment. 'Duane, I'd be sorry to lose you. You're a fine driver. But if you feel that this is what you should be doing, I would never stand in your way. Sure, you can leave when you want to.

'And, Duane,' he added as an afterthought, 'I wish you all the luck in the world.'

I hadn't the heart to tell him that I didn't believe in luck any more.

Now came an even bigger hurdle. We had to sell our home and furniture. I quickly formulated an advertisement for the local newspaper and dropped it into the office, people at our church also knew that we wanted to sell the property.

Before the newspaper ad had even appeared, a knock came at our front door. There stood a middle-aged man.

'Ma'am,' he said to Carole, 'I've been informed that this home might be for sale.'

Carole was staggered.

'Well, it certainly could be. We are hoping to go to South Carolina so that my husband can study to go into the ministry.'

His eyes lit up. 'That's great news. You see, I'm a Christian. Someone from your church told me you might be selling your home. Ma'am, I've driven past here so many times and admired the house. Could I bring my wife back here in the morning so she can look at it?'

They came back the next day—and bought it for cash.

Everything went to them, including the furniture.

Within four days of our talking to John, we were off. Carole and I loaded what we had been able to pack in boxes and suitcases into a trailer I had been given. The last item I put in was my box of plumbing tools.

'I'll probably be needing those for work in Greenville,' I told Carole.

We had already said farewell to our friends at church, and parked outside Pastor Yaxley's home for a final goodbye. It was Tuesday morning, August 23rd, 1953, as we gathered in a circle with the pastor and his wife for a farewell prayer. Then Pastor Yaxley turned to us and said, 'Remember, God was faithful to Abraham and Sarah who went to a land they knew not of. He will also be faithful to you in the same way.'

With that we all kissed and hugged and then climbed into my 1941 car, with trailer fully loaded, for the long trip south east and a new life.

As we sped along, climbing higher and higher out of the Skagit Valley, I found many emotions swirling within me. Was I really doing God's will, or was this a crazy idea that I had psyched myself into? I turned and looked at my two young boys, so excited with the prospect of their new life.

But I couldn't forget what Carole's father had said to me when I told him of our move. 'You're crazy,' he had snapped. 'Do you realize what you are doing? You are taking my daughter and grandchildren right across America with nowhere to live and hardly any money to support them. Duane Logsdon, all I can say to you is, "You're nuts!"'

Maybe I was. Only time would tell.

# CHAPTER EIGHT

# Spiders and Snakes

'Help, there's a snake in here! Help, please somebody help me!' Carole's terror-stricken voice rose several decibels.

Daryl and Bob, two neighbours in the shabby trailer park, nicknamed 'Tar Paper Shack Town', where we now lived in Greenville, came running armed with a hoe and sticks to kill the creepy reptile that fell from the rafter first on to Carole's shoulder and then to the floor.

'It's there, under the stove. It's at least six feet long!' Carole's legs felt hollow. Prickly heat like a thousand needles jabbed at her body.

A neighbour called me from the 'restrooms' that were about half a block from our small trailer, where I had been doing a minor plumbing job. I came running to find Carole standing petrified as Daryl fished around under the stove and managed to pull out, by the tail, a six-inch baby bull snake.

'Don't worry, Carole, it won't eat you,' chuckled Bob as he threw it outside and then chopped it in two with his hoe.

'I'm sorry,' she sobbed in apology, 'but you know that I just can't stand snakes. To have one in the house with the two boys terrified me.'

It had taken us a total of six days of hard driving to reach Greenville, the city we believed to be our

Promised Land. The journey had been particularly hard for all of us—Carole, the two kids, Donnie nearly three, David thirteen months, and a young man named Guy Morris, who was going back to Bob Jones University to begin his preparation for the ministry.

Our first night was spent in a cheap motel in Eastern Washington. The next morning Carole went into the adjoining bedroom to check on the boys, when she let out a cry.

'Duane, come here! David's missing!'

I came running in to find Carole in a state of panic, David was nowhere to be found.

We began searching the premises, the car park, and the car, but there was no sign of him.

'Did you see David get up and leave?' I asked Don.

'No, Daddy, I don't know where he is.'

Finally I walked back into the motel, and I had a brainwave.

'Have you looked under the bed?' I asked Carole.

She hadn't. There he was, curled up in a little ball, covered by a blanket, and sucking his thumb. For a long time she just stood and stared at our son, a small grinning replica of Carole.

'I fell down, Mummy,' he explained, giving her a smile that would melt any parent's heart.

We loaded up and were back on the road, this time to Casper, Wyoming. About ten miles before arriving, I heard an ominous clunk at the back of the car. I pulled off the road to find that the left rear spring leaf on the trailer had broken.

'We'll have to inch our way into town and see if we can find a replacement, but the chances are very slim. This is a home-made trailer.

'Let's ask God to do a miracle here. Otherwise we are in big trouble.' We each bowed our heads and I prayed, asking God to intervene for us.

As we were gingerly bumping along, we finally reached Casper. 'Look, there's a wrecking yard up ahead,' Guy said, straining to see through the glare of the windscreen. I went in to see if they had a replacement leaf spring.

'What kind of chassis does your trailer have, sir?' the proprietor asked, thoughtfully sucking on his pipe.

'I don't know, you'll have to come out and see.'

He soon discovered the type of frame the trailer had, and went back in and dug around the mounds of parts. He finally found exactly what I needed, a used main leaf.

I paid him, dug out my tool box, jacked the trailer up and proceeded to instal the spring.

One hour and forty-five minutes later the job was completed. I quickly washed my hands, and we continued on towards the city that was 'flowing with milk and honey'.

The next day, our little bunch merrily continued on our marathon journey. At about three in the afternoon the sun was beating down mercilessly; the kids were hot and weary, but we knew we had to keep going.

Suddenly I heard a heavy knock coming from inside the engine and then I saw, to my horror, the oil gauge pressure rapidly dropping to the danger level.

I stopped and opened the bonnet, and realized that we were in deep trouble again. We were losing our connecting rod bearings and we were still a hundred miles from our next stop, where Carole's grandparents lived.

As I got back into the car, I told Carole and Guy, 'The only thing we can do is to ask God to perform another miracle to keep this jalopy running until we get there. It really shouldn't go another inch, let alone another hundred miles.'

We bowed our heads, and asked the Lord once again to prove himself to us in our desperate situation.

I started the engine and cautiously drove on, watching the oil needle. To my utter amazement it shot up and the car ran reasonably well. We covered the entire distance without any further problems.

Upon arrival in Albany, where Carole's grandparents lived, I unhooked the trailer and drove to the corner service station and asked the tobacco-chewing owner if I might drive my car up on the ramp to repair the engine.

'I'm the grandson of Arch and Sadie Summa,' I told the little, round-faced man.

'Well, young'un,' he said, 'I'll be happy to supply you with anything that will help you out of your predicament.'

The air was heavy and humid as I removed the oil sump and dismantled the bearing caps. To my amazement, they were so scorched and battered, that actually, the car shouldn't have gone five miles—let alone one hundred! I turned to Guy and said, 'God's done it again. What a miracle.'

We hurriedly walked across the town square to a spare-parts supplier, and found that they had the very bearings we needed. Within a short time my old car, purring like a kitten, was back on the road.

*     *     *

*Welcome to Greenville*. The sign greeted us just as we came up over the hill. At last we had made it to the city we had looked forward to with such anticipation. We felt welcome.

I turned and said to our gang, with tears in my eyes,

'Mission accomplished!' We were all aware that what God had started, he planned to continue.

Carole smiled wearily and said, 'This city looks like a beautiful place, Duane. I think we're going to be very happy here.'

I drove on for a few more miles until we reached the eastern section of the city, and suddenly we saw spread out ahead of us the campus of Bob Jones University. The Rodeheaver Auditorium stood on the brow of a hill and the campus was set amidst trees and beautiful grounds. All the buildings were painted a cream colour.

We drove through the entrance gates and parked in front of the administration building. I asked Carole to wait in the car while Guy and I went to report in.

As we entered the building I felt all my exhaustion melt away. My face was alive with excitement, and a bounce came into my step.

A girl student, her face flashing a warm smile, sat at the registration desk. She looked as neatly manicured as the grounds outside. I introduced myself and explained that we were checking in for pre-registration. After filling out the necessary card, I asked her if she could give me some direction regarding housing for students, explaining that we were a family of four, and Guy would be a dorm student.

'Well, Mr Logsdon,' she said, spreading her hands, 'several of the married students live in trailer parks around here. There's one just across the motorway. Also, there is one called University Student Homes behind the girls' dorm. There may be something suitable in either place.'

Because it was easier to go to the park behind the girls' dorm, due to traffic congestion, I turned the car to the right and parked in front of the run-down trailer site. As I got out of the car, I was approached by a short, friendly man who extended a hand and said, 'Hi, my name is Tom Shea. I bet you're a new student coming in.'

'Yes, that's right. We're looking for a place to live.'

He explained that a couple, just leaving the university, had a place for sale. 'It's just down the walk on the right.'

Then, as a family, we walked until we saw the 'For Sale' sign on the sky-blue trailer. I knocked at the door.

A man with dark hair, and a baby cradled in his arms, opened the door. His name was Ivan. I explained that we had been told his place was for sale.

'It sure is. I have finished my work at summer school. My wife Pat is just finishing her student-teaching and we feel the Lord is leading us to Alaska to work as missionaries.'

We soon got down to basics and Ivan said it was mine, fully furnished, for 'just $400'. It consisted of a little twenty-eight foot trailer that was twenty years old, with a small add-on room big enough to hold a sofa, a chair and an oil stove.

Ivan showed us through the crumbling, uncarpeted trailer, and even though it had no plumbing or bathroom facilities, I felt this was our new home.

Within an hour we had shaken hands on a deal and, because Ivan and his wife had another trailer on the site which they were going to take with them to Alaska, we were able to move in that very night.

We unloaded as much of our belongings as we could, and then set up the kitchen. Carole prepared beds, and then explored the area. We found that the laundry room and bathroom facilities were about 200 yards away. Guy's things were unloaded and he was established in the dorm.

'What do you think of the place?' I asked Carole. Her face said it all. 'It's terrible. But if this is where God wants us to live, I'll have to get used to it.'

Exhausted, we dropped onto our beds and, despite the sour-smelling air, slipped off into a deep sleep.

In the middle of the night David woke us all up, screaming like mad. I went rushing to him on the couch.

He was sobbing in terror and pointing at a huge spider that had run across his covers and then quickly disappeared under the screen door.

I looked at Carole and then little David who was still heaving great sobs.

'Oh well,' she sighed, 'it could have been worse; it might have been a snake. . . .'

# CHAPTER NINE

# 'Do Right Till the Stars Fall'

Dr Bob Jones hitched up his trousers, mopped his brow with a handkerchief and took up a dramatic stance, facing head-on the 3,000 students in front of him.

'Do right till the stars fall,' he boomed out, his jaw tightening for a moment. 'Dr Bob', as he liked to be called, didn't need a microphone.

'You can borrow brains, but you can't borrow character,' he added in that distinctive southern accent that somehow also seemed to contain a slight hint of a Boston drawl.

I felt a tingle up my spine as I listened for the first time to this old warhorse with his uniquely American brand of fundamentalism. His spellbinding presentation made it easy for me to understand why he was first licensed to preach at the age of fifteen, and had spoken at evangelistic crusades all around the world.

As we hung on his every word, I recalled how his friend, Billy Sunday, had once declared, 'Bob Jones has the wit of Sam Jones; the homely philosophy of George Stuart; the eloquence of Sam Small; and the spiritual fervency of Dwight L. Moody.'

Dr Bob enjoyed quoting his homespun philosophies. And so that we wouldn't forget them, many of the 'sayings of Dr Bob' festooned the walls of the university.

After a few minutes of his unique 'wisdom' and a sermon from the word, he again faced us full on.

'Finally,' he said, filling the Rodeheaver Auditorium with his voice, 'I want to welcome all of you to the *world's most unusual university*.'

I suppose there really was some basis for Dr Bob's claim. For, while this was undoubtedly a Christian institution, there was also a great emphasis on the fine arts. The university had a magnificent cinema department, as well as a top-drawer drama section that presented some of Shakespeare's greatest plays. It also had a wonderful biblical and archaeological museum.

The academic standards were very high, but Dr Bob also made sure that all students were involved in personal evangelism.

The adage that 'cleanliness is next to godliness' prevailed throughout the campus. Everyone was expected to be neat, and many of the male students had crew cuts; it was thought by them to be a required-part of their Bob Jones University 'uniform'.

As we filed out of that first chapel service of the term, a fellow student told me proudly, 'Do you know that this university has the largest group of men in the country who are preparing for the ministry? Dr Bob calls us the 'Preacher Boys'. I'm one of them you know!'

I looked suitably impressed and held out my hand to congratulate him.

'So am I, friend,' I told him to his surprise. 'So am I.'

The days that followed merged like the pages of a book into a phrenetic round of dashing from class to class and getting used to the regimentation of life on campus. Not having studied for some five years, I found myself swamped by all the information that I was expected to retain.

I would return 'home' at night to find Carole look-ing equally flustered after a day in our 'tar paper shack' trying to manage the kids, cook, and keep the trailer in some semblance of order. One night I noticed that her face was stamped with pain and her eyes dark with concern. 'What's up, Carole?' I asked, as I gently touched her hand and smiled at her. 'Have the kids been getting you down again?'

'Well, partly. But that's not my main problem.'

She paused as if unable to tell me the next news. Then she blurted out, 'Look, Duane, we've just about run out of money. The cash we got for the sale of the house and furniture is almost gone.'

I had forgotten little things like our cash flow situa-tion. My studies and the excitement of my new life had just about overwhelmed me.

I put my arm around Carole. 'Don't worry, darling,' I said in a soothing tone. 'The answer lies in my tool box. Let's pray that the Lord will help me get some plumbing opportunities really soon.'

A few days later I was shaving at our kitchen sink when a man came and knocked at the door.

'Say neighbour,' he said in a friendly tone, 'is it true that you are a plumber?'

I nodded and winced as I nicked my chin.

'Are you good?'

'Sure am,' wiping the blood from my cut with a paper towel. *The best I know.*'

'Great, I may have a job for you. I'm a brick mason and I'm working for a Christian guy who needs some-one to plumb a house for him. It could lead to lots of other work.'

Next day I drove out to the beautiful home of his boss, Jim Pitts. After hearing of my background, a smile lit up his face.

'Son,' he said, as we sat in his spacious living room splashed with autumn sunshine, 'you just may be the answer to my prayers. I have a particular job that needs doing right away, and if you do it well, there could be others.'

I explained that my studies kept me busy weekdays. 'I suppose I could work evenings and Saturdays though.' I then looked straight at him. 'Sir, I feel just like Abraham in a new land. I really believe that God, through you, has proved faithful in his provision for me and my family.'

*     *     *

'Mummy, can I have a biscuit?' 'Can I go outside and play?' 'Mummy, I've got to go potty.' The constant demands of the two children had begun to get to Carole.

Finally, one morning as I was in class, she snapped like a twig. 'Mummy, Mummy, Mummy,' she screamed, 'if I hear that one more time, I'll go crazy.' She began sobbing deep, heartfelt sobs.

'Can't you kids find something to do and leave me alone?' she shouted, wet eyed and emotional.

Our mobile home had become like a prison cell for Carole. I was usually only there at night to sleep, what with my studies and work. And when I did finally stagger in bleary-eyed, I was too tired to talk.

One afternoon, in sheer desperation, Carole told God of her utter frustration. 'Lord, you know the thing I want most is to be the person you want me to be, the wife you want me to be, and the mother you want me to be, but I know that I'm blowing it all. I can't take much more.'

But even as she talked with the Lord, Carole had a

feeling that he was not really listening, or even interested.

Although each day I saw the strain and tension written all over my wife's face, struggling as she was within the confinements of our trailer home, I somehow could not identify with her problems. I guess it was because I was so bowed down myself with the heavy pressure of my studies and work.

I was so grateful to have work, though I knew the money I was earning was not much. Almost every day we were faced with yet another financial crisis, like the time Don, by now three, opened the valve on a neighbour's fuel oil barrel and all the fuel oil drained out onto the ground. That meant we had to compensate the couple concerned with money we just couldn't afford to part with at that time.

Our eating habits, too, were frugal. Often we would make our way to the Cash 'n Carry market and pay five cents each for unlabelled, dented cans. We would shake them to try and guess what was in them. Eventually we became quite skilled and could usually tell if carrots were in there or string beans. The climactic moment came when we got home and prepared for the ceremonial opening.

'Ah ha, right again, it *is* green beans,' Carole would triumphantly exclaim. We weren't always right, however, and we would then be stuck with food we didn't really fancy.

Another way we would 'chance' our money would be at shops where we could purchase day-old bakery goods. When we got back we would excitedly dig around in the bags to see how much bread was in there along with the biscuits and cupcakes.

One day, it suddenly dawned on me that if Carole could be freed from some of this confinement, it would be helpful to her. I approached Al Carter, the manager of the trailer park. He said he could certainly offer her some employment.

'Maybe she could start by collecting rents for the spaces the mobile homes occupy,' he told us, as Carole and I stood in his shabby office. 'Maybe then she could manage the laundry facilities. If Carole did that, I'd be happy to let you use the washing machines for free!'

But the euphoria of her new responsibility didn't last long. I returned home one evening after attending a 'Spiritual Life Emphasis' meeting at the university, at which I had really been challenged about my service for God. I wanted to share this with Carole and tell her how I had made a fresh commitment to God to serve him with every fibre of my being. I felt wonderfully renewed.

I sailed excitedly through the door wanting to tell my wife I had also been challenged about the lack of depth in my prayer life. As I began to share this with Carole, I hadn't really noticed the anguish on her face.

'I think I'll go to my secret place of prayer in the woods behind the trailer park,' I told her. Whenever I went to this little spot, even in the dark, I would glimpse heaven there. I would talk to God as the wind talked to the trees.

To my utter amazement and shock, Carole suddenly interrupted the flow of my conversation. She shook her head and sighed hopelessly and then released a pent-up flood of emotion. 'Go to your old meadow,' she snapped. 'I don't care! Stay as long as you like!'

Then she added in a desperate tone that indicated her life was coming apart at the seams, 'When you come back you probably won't find me here. I'm leaving!' her lower lip trembled, her eyes were flooded by tears.

I just stared at her; I felt devastated. Carole had suddenly 'dropped the axe'. There was a cold knot in the pit of my stomach. I felt she was no longer my helpmate, but an enemy.

Confused and taken aback, I turned on my heel and left the trailer, muttering, 'I'll be back.' Whether Carole would still be there, however, I had no idea.

I knelt in the darkened meadow with tears streaming down my face and a stream of emotion welling up within me.

'Lord, you know that we are not here by our choice, but by yours! But how can I stay without Carole?' I found it hard to even speak the words. 'Lord, whatever you want me to do, I'm willing to do it.'

I laid this confusing problem at God's feet.

'Please work in her heart and help her through this terrible time,' I asked God. 'This situation is beyond me.'

Little did I realize that while I was praying, God was already beginning to answer my prayer.

For even then, a drama was being enacted back in our trailer.

*   *   *

'I'm sick, Mummy.' David's face was flushed, almost red hot.

'Well, what's wrong with you?' Carole snapped, still feeling angry with herself and God.

'I'm hot, I feel I'm on fire.'

When Carole dampened a cloth and went to wash his face, she noticed how badly he was burning up with fever. She took his temperature and found it to be 104·5°F.

'Oh God,' she urgently prayed as she sank to her

knees, 'please stop this fever, and . . . please forgive me for becoming so bitter about my situation. And for hurting Duane. I've really been walking in the flesh.'

I came in as Carole was still kneeling at the side of our bed where David lay, desperately sick. I gently put my hand on her shoulder and then got down beside her and kissed away the tears that had welled up in her eyes.

After Carole had finished her anguished prayer, I took over.

'Lord,' I implored him, my voice shaking, 'I want Carole and I to truly rededicate our lives to you. Please God, touch little David's body and heal him of this illness.'

As we stood up, David suddenly sat up. 'Mummy,' he exclaimed, rubbing his eyes as if he had been asleep, 'Can I have some toys? I want to play.'

Carole reached down to touch his forehead and discovered that his temperature had instantaneously come down. For a long moment she just stared at me.

'Duane,' she finally blurted out, 'I am sorry for upsetting you. I suppose Dr Bob's saying, "Do right till the stars fall," is right after all. I haven't been doing right by you and the kids lately. There's no excuse. I want to support you all I can from now on.'

She paused and a smile spread across her lips. 'I really want to support you, Duane. . . .'

I took her hand . . . 'till the stars fall . . . is that right, honey?'

# CHAPTER TEN

# Argie's Service

'Hey, Argie,' I said, heartily slapping him on the back, 'how about closing up this old place of yours and joining me for a week of meetings?'

'Duane!' he exclaimed with delight, countering my question with his own. 'What are you doing here?'

Argie Blackburn's overalls were streaked with oil and grease, but that didn't stop him from throwing his arms around me and giving me a bear-hug.

'Hey, stop that,' I tried to protest. 'You'll ruin my one and only suit.'

I was back in Mount Vernon, with Carole and the boys for the summer break of 1954, after completing my first year at Bob Jones University. Carole's parents had loaned us their home so we could enjoy our time with our friends, without worrying about accommodation. I hadn't been there very long when Ken Wymer, a former Skagit Valley boy who was now pastor of the First Baptist Church of Colville, a wheat town in our state, invited me to lead an evangelistic crusade at his church. I was delighted to accept, but knew I needed a team to join me.

I immediately thought of Argie as song-leader and tenor soloist. This red-haired, square-jawed, friend had been a Mobil Oil lorry driver at the same time I had been. He now owned his own service station, *Argie's Service*. When we had been deliverymen together, Argie and I often used to visit the bars.

Shortly after my conversion, I met him on the street.

'Hey, Duane,' he greeted me, and chuckled. 'Is it true that you've seen the light? Surely a renegade like you wouldn't go for all that religious stuff.' He made a face of simulated disapproval. 'How about joining me for a pint tonight?'

I countered that with my own suggestion. 'Argie, I've got a better proposal. There are some special services at our church this week. Why not come with me instead? If you hate it, you can walk out. I wouldn't be upset.'

His brow furrowed, and he brushed a fleck of ash from his tie. I pressed him further and finally he reluctantly agreed.

'I'll come just for old times' sake,' he said, adding a warning, 'but don't expect me to get saved, or anything crazy like that.'

At that night's meeting I sat next to Argie. He shifted in his seat most of the time as for the first time he heard about the love of God and the awful reality of hell for anyone who rejected that love. I found myself praying urgently for Argie as the altar call was made. Slowly, at first, but then with determination, he stood up and went to the front of the church. There, with a group of others, he prayed the 'sinner's prayer' and turned over his life to God.

That evening, a re-run of Carole's conversion took place at Argie's home, when Grace Yaxley went around to talk to his lovely wife, Pat. She too accepted Christ into her life. Under Pastor Yaxley's ministry Argie and Pat grew quickly as Christians. Argie soon became the church song leader and his tenor solos became the talk of the congregation.

Now, here I was, just one year later with my 'brother

in Christ'. Argie quickly consulted his staff and they assured him that he wouldn't need to close up; they'd take care of the business while he was away.

'Okay, Duane, you've talked me into it,' he finally told me.

We told Pastor Yaxley of our plans and he rather surprisingly agreed to allow his daughter Roberta to join us as crusade pianist. Each night the sanctuary of the church in Colville was packed to capacity as Argie led the singing and then, with Roberta accompanying him, sang a couple of gospel favourites. I would then preach and, at the close, invite people to give their lives to Jesus Christ. It was an exciting time for all of us as people came forward.

On Wednesday night we had a wonderful meeting and, after my sermon, people again came forward. Argie as usual led the singing of the invitation hymn, 'Is Your All on the Altar?' I turned to look at him from the pulpit where I stood, and couldn't understand why he kept dabbing his eyes with a handkerchief.

'It must be the emotion of seeing people giving their lives over to God,' I thought.

Back in the dreary motel room we shared, I asked Argie why he had been weeping during the invitation.

'Duane, it wasn't only because of the new converts.'

I was puzzled. 'Well, what was it then, Argie?'

'It was . . .' he paused for a moment, as if not quite sure how to explain his feelings. Then he let it all pour out.

'It was because I know that I am a fraud. You see I know my *all* is not on the altar for God. I have let *Argie's Service* be my security instead of letting go and letting God. . . .'

'Are you saying that God is calling you into the ministry?' I asked Argie as he knelt at his bedside.

'That's it, Duane, I'm sure that's it.'

I knelt at his side and told him to go ahead and tell God everything.

'Lord,' he said, after a few minutes, 'I'm willing to give up my business and surrender my very life to you. I want my *all* on the altar for Jesus Christ. Wherever *you* want me to go, I'll go.'

Argie's commitment that night had widespread repercussions that soon found Argie and Pat following us to Bob Jones University, and then eventually serving in the pastorate of four churches. It also reached into the very heart of the rock movement in the late sixties.

For in 1970, while Argie was pastor of Dunlap Baptist Church in South Central Seattle, he was asked to conduct the funeral for the controversial black rock guitarist, Jimi Hendrix, who had died on September 18th, choking on vomit caused by a barbiturate overdose in London, England.

After Hendrix, known to many as the Wild Man of Rock, was found dead at his girlfriend's apartment, a minister made an astonishing attack on him. Writing in a British Christian newspaper, the pastor claimed Hendrix had 'disintegrated the lives of teenagers'. He said he was an alcoholic, a drug addict and grossly promiscuous. 'Far from being a great musician—he was a veritable destroyer.'

The pastor said that Hendrix's 'mind sounds' had caused some young people to collapse in a psychological heap. He even declared that many parents lost their teenage girls completely because of the influence of this 'so-called musician'.

At the end of his stinging attack, the minister said, 'It is no accident that Jimi Hendrix died at the age of twenty-four looking like a man twice as old.'

Argie had possibly a more understanding view of this tormented young man.

He later told me, 'They flew his body over to Seattle and, because my church was in the area he came from, his grieving family asked me to conduct the funeral service and the later internment.

'It was an incredible experience, with weeping and screaming Hendrix fans crowding outside the church and then coming to the cemetery. There were television crews from around the world covering the services.

'I had a chance to share the gospel of Jesus with those at the funeral. It was a unique opportunity. Guess who was among the mourners at the service? John Lennon, the ex-Beatle who was later murdered in New York. So he also heard all about the Lord that day!'

I smiled, 'Well, Argie, I guess it *was* a good move for you when you gave up *Argie's Service* for *"Argie's Higher Service".'*

He grinned. 'Duane, I'm not going to argue with you.'

*   *   *

Carole sank into the chair opposite me and nervously fingered the upholstery. It was autumn 1954 and we were back in our mobile home in Greenville. Once again I was deeply involved in my studies and outside plumbing work. It seemed, at last, that I was bringing in almost enough money to support our family of four. It was a struggle, but not as tough as during much of our first year.

'What's wrong, Carole?' I said as a tear spilled over the curve of one eye and slipped down her cheek. 'You look as if you've been given some bad news.'

Carole dabbed at her eyes with a handkerchief. Her delicate face had turned deathly pale.

'Well, Duane, it depends how you look at it.' Then she blurted it out. 'You're going to be a daddy again next February.'

I felt I had been hit by a sledgehammer. I knew that Carole was not really physically strong enough to bear a third child and my income was not enough to cope with this extra expense.

'Carole, why has God done this to us? Doesn't he realize the problems we already have?' My voice was high and despairing.

'But Duane . . .' She looked at me in frank surprise.

I felt a dark anger well up in me. Here I was, serving God in difficult circumstances, and he seemed to be repaying me by making my life even more trying. I experienced a feeling of desertion.

'Carole, I'm going to bed. I can't stand any more of this.' I shook my head and sighed hopelessly.

Usually, before I went to sleep, I would sink to my knees and spend some time in prayer and praise before the Lord. But this night I was so angry that I just undressed and slumped into bed.

Next day, during my classes, I could hardly keep my mind on what the professors were saying. I had unwillingly fallen prey to bitterness. All I wanted to do was argue with God.

'Why are you giving me such a hard time?' I asked the Almighty, pumped up with outrage. 'Here I am working my fingers to the bone, hardly able to feed my family now, so how can I support another one?'

That Saturday I was expected by the University to be part of an outreach team going to the town of Pickens, South Carolina. We were a tight-knit team of young men, and it had become tradition that I drove everyone there in my car.

That Saturday, in a fit of pique, I didn't see why it always had to be my car. After the usual period of prayer, the three men went and got into my car.

I stood in front of it and said, 'Hey, I'm sick of having to take my car and pay for the petrol.' And I added loudly, 'Let's go in one of yours.'

They looked at me frankly disbelieving and exchanged uneasy looks. 'But we always go in yours,' protested Ken, his face tightening.

'Yes, that's the problem,' I snapped, my temper burning on a short fuse. 'None of you ever chip in for the expenses. I just can't afford it any more.'

So we climbed into Ken's car and, after arriving at the town, went on the streets to witness. I had no joy whatever that day, but just went through the operation mechanically.

'How did it go?' asked Peter, one of the young men, as we drove back to Greenville after several hours on the streets.

'Oh, I bagged two scalps,' I remarked, my voice dripping with sarcasm.

'Is that how you look at those people who made commitments?' he asked as his eyes peeled me open.

I said nothing, but proffered a smile as hard as a car grill. I had enough troubles without getting into an argument with fellow students.

My attendance at the local Brethren church began to slip as well. Although I had for the previous year been an enthusiastic regular, I found that I now had no desire to go to the services. I would sleep in on Sunday mornings and, if I was really pushed, go to the little evening service organized by students living in the trailer park.

Gradually, a nightmare was beginning to envelop me like an impenetrable fog. 'If you don't care for me, why should I get all excited about going to church?' I would shout at God.

Then a new dimension came into my bitterness. I was finding my secular studies increasingly difficult to cope with. I wondered if I should have tried to take on science, maths, history and art, when I could have gone to a Bible school and just concentrated on that *one* subject. My studies, my plumbing work, and the thought of another mouth to feed became a black cloud pressing down on my spirit which would not go away.

The months dragged by, but the bitterness didn't. It was now late January 1955 and the baby was due soon.

Then came further complications.

One day, as Carole lay in bed at home, I went to her and held her hand.

'Honey', I told her dejectedly, 'I hate to unload another worry on you, but I've just realized that unless I am able to pay our bill at the university hospital, I will probably not be able to sign up for my middle term. I would then be excluded from any further studies. It's university policy, and I don't have the money to pay!'

Carole looked at me and burst into tears. She rocked back and forth on the bed, her head in her hands.

'When will all of this end?' she sobbed. 'I don't think I can take much more.'

Just days before the baby was due, a knock came on the front door. Carole went and opened it and was confronted with the smiling face of her mother, Juanita.

'I've come to help,' she beamed. They had flown all the way from Seattle.

Carole burst into tears and slammed the door. She ran to her bedroom and threw herself on the bed, weeping uncontrollably. She felt wretched and miserable. Her mother let herself in and came and quietly put her arm around her daughter. 'What's the problem, dear? I thought you'd be pleased to see me.'

'But mother, I didn't want you to see the degrading way in which we live. It's so humiliating!'

*     *     *

It was the morning of February 18th, 1955, and I left for my classes as usual. I knew the time for the birth was close, so I asked Carole to make sure that if anything happened, someone from the university office would let me know.

I had been in class for only thirty minutes, when the message came.

'Mr Logsdon, your wife has been rushed to the delivery room.'

I ran as fast as I could through the grounds to the hospital. I was greeted by a nurse who informed me that the baby had come quickly and I was now the father of a $9\frac{1}{2}$lb boy.

'Mother and baby are doing fine,' she added brightly. 'If you will wait just a few minutes, Mr Logsdon, you'll be able to see them both.'

At that moment I felt a new warmth invading my being, a feeling of calm and peace. A rekindling of my commitment. I realized that God had given us a wonderful gift, not a crushing burden. I also felt a sick disgust about my recent bitterness and anger towards him.

'Lord, I am sorry for my behaviour,' I said, wanting forgiveness. 'I've been a real heel. I don't care if I do get thrown out of Bob Jones. The important thing is that I get right again with you.'

As I walked through the door into the small room where Carole was sitting up in bed with our son, whom we later named Daniel Dean. I kissed her and then picked up the little bundle of life and held him in my hands.

As little Danny struggled valiantly to cope with his brand-new life, I said to Carole, 'Do you realize what day this is?'

Exhaustion was written all over her face, but my question still provoked a broad smile.

'Yes,' I remember. 'It's our third spiritual birthday. Just three years ago we both handed our lives over to God.'

'What a day for our new son to be born. It's certainly a triple birthday.' I was ecstatic.

The nurse soon ushered me out of the ward, saying that Carole needed to rest. I blew her a kiss and gently closed the door.

I thought I would walk across to the local post office to see if there was any mail. I could see through the window at our post office box that there was an envelope there. I dialled the combination and reached in to pull it out.

It bore a Mount Vernon postmark. I was always glad to hear from friends in my hometown. I quickly opened it and found that it contained a note and a money order.

I read the note which said, 'We the Eternal Builders Class of Emmanuel Baptist Church felt that you might be in need at this time and have taken up a love offering for you and Carole. Please forgive the cents as there was some loose change but we decided to send you everything that was collected.'

My eyes began to brim with tears when I saw the total amount. It was $59.46, which to my amazement was the exact amount of the medical bill I had been presented with by the hospital for the birth of our baby.

I found myself praying involuntarily.

'Lord,' I said, hoarsely, 'please forgive me for my rebellious spirit and lack of faith over these past few months. All I can say is, I am sorry, and thank you.'

I was later allowed back in the ward with Carole and Daniel, and we wept together as I shared with her what had happened at the mail box.

'Duane,' she turned to me and clasped my hand, 'isn't it wonderful that God would do such things for us on our spiritual birthdays?

'We didn't deserve to be entrusted with a new life, but still he gave it to us.' She broke into a smile so powerful that it filled out her cheeks and drew attention to her lively, hazel eyes.

'Yes, you're right,' I replied, unable to suppress a smile. 'I guess we didn't deserve salvation as well. But he still gave it to us.'

# CHAPTER ELEVEN

# To March or Not to March

A sharp dart of pain shot up my right leg and my face twisted in agony. It was nearly midnight and I was working on my own on an urgent plumbing job.

I was nine feet off the ground when the scaffolding suddenly gave way. I gasped as I felt myself falling downwards, almost in slow motion, but my tiredness prevented me from doing anything to help myself.

As I lay on the floor of this partly completed shop in Greenville, I began muttering hoarsely to myself, 'You dummy, you dummy!'

I knew that graduation at Bob Jones was just six weeks away and here I was with what was almost certainly a broken leg.

'Lord, how will I be able to walk down the aisle to receive my degree if it's really broken? This is terrible. I've been here for four gruelling years, now this happens.' I was overwhelmed with a sense of helplessness.

In the pale illumination of two stark, bare light bulbs hanging from the ceiling, I managed to grab hold of a metal scaffolding pole and pull myself up to a standing position. I knew I had to go on, so I gritted my teeth and worked on for another agonizing hour. I was soaked in sweat and my muscles ached. I gathered up my tools and hobbled out to my car. I was exhausted, wretched and miserable.

I turned the ignition key and the engine spluttered into laborious life. I gasped with pain as I gingerly pressed my foot against the accelerator. My white-knuckled hands gripped the steering wheel and I slowly moved off, homeward bound.

When I got back, Carole was in a deep sleep, so I undressed and eased myself into the bed beside her. I lay back and closed my eyes, hoping that sleep would come and wipe away the throbbing pain. But it didn't.

At about 3.00 a.m. I couldn't lie there any longer. I threw off the covers and almost fell out of bed. On my hands and knees I crawled to the cupboard-size bathroom I had recently built onto our mobile home and was violently sick. Then my world went grey and I toppled backwards, like an axed tree, cracking my head first on the wall, then the floor.

The sudden noise caused Carole to wake up with a start. She shook me to try and wake me up.

I felt my eyes open for just a split second and saw a brief flash of panic on her face. 'Carole,' I moaned, 'I'm really ill. I need help.'

A student neighbour, who had medical training, was roused, and he immediately helped Carole drag me back to bed. He gave me some pain-killing tablets and, with my brain temporarily deprogrammed, I slept fitfully until 5.00 a.m. when I awoke again. I saw to my horror that my right leg, just above the ankle, had swollen to twice its previous size.

Carole drove me to see an orthopaedic doctor for a nine o'clock appointment. He carefully examined my leg, and then shook his head when I told him that after I had fallen from the scaffolding I had worked on for another hour.

'Good grief, man, are you completely mad?' was his horrified response.

I shook my head.

'Don't you realize you've broken a bone? That work you so foolishly did has made it even worse. That's why it has swollen up like a balloon.'

The doctor set the bone the best he could, but wasn't able to put a full cast on because of the size of the swelling.

'Mr Logsdon, you must not stand on that leg for at least a week. By then the swelling should have gone down and I'll recast it.'

As Carole drove me home, I turned to her and said, This really is going to cause me a lot of problems. If I don't finish this particular job, all the other sub-contractors will suffer, because they won't be able to complete their work. Then there is the Bible conference at the University which I really should attend. In fact, it's compulsory.'

The doctor had given me crutches, so that night I managed to hobble from the car into the Bible conference. But all the way through, I kept thinking that my accident was going to cause real difficulty for others on the site.

Finally, I decided that I would go back to complete the work. I had a helper, Kenneth Shell, who also lived in the trailer park, and I asked him to get ready for a long night.

'Duane, please don't go,' Carole begged. 'You'll only make things worse.'

I knew she was right, but I also felt responsible to complete my part of the contract. That night my whole body ached as I limped around the site, running water lines and repairing leaks in some of the pipes. As I crawled along the floor, saturated in water, I could feel the water seeping into my plaster cast. Soon my whole body became chilled as the wind whistled and howled and moaned through the shell of the building.

Not surprisingly the pain soon came again, in throbbing waves. It was indescribable. Exhausted and weary, Kenneth helped me back to the car. The taut lines in my face indicated to him that things were far from right.

That night in bed the pain in my right leg became even more intense. The next morning it was so bad I asked Carole to drive me back to the doctor.

'I know I should really report at the university office and tell them, but really this is an emergency!' My face was still twisted in agony.

The doctor was horrified when he saw the shape my cast was in.

'You must be out of your mind,' he remarked as I told him how I had worked late the previous night. 'Your cast has disintegrated and you have been moving about on a broken bone.'

This time he put on a plaster cast.

'Now try and rest as much as you can, but if you must work, at least the water won't ruin the cast.'

Back at our mobile home, Carole made me a sandwich. As I rested my leg on a soft stool, she explained how excited she was that we had both survived the four years in Greenville, and how we had seen God provide for us.

'You know,' she grinned, 'even that turkey-filling in your sandwich is another of God's miracles.'

I smiled back. I knew what she meant. For months now we had been struggling with a food problem. Although my work provided me with a reasonably good income, I had found that there was hardly any left for food. So we began praying together for help.

'Now, Lord,' I prayed one day, 'you promised to supply all our needs in Christ Jesus, and you know it's been a month since we had a taste of meat.'

Not wanting to tell others of our needs, because we were too proud, we never shared our situation with them. Later that day, after going to check our mail box, we returned to find our doorway piled high with groceries.

Neighbours had waited for us to leave for a few minutes and then sneaked in with their gifts. It seemed that God had told them that we were in need of food. This happened on numerous other occasions too.

As I ate the sandwich, I turned to Carole and said, 'Elijah was fed by the ravens, and God has used our neighbours to answer our prayers and supply us with food.'

Although I found it very hard at times to 'prove' God, I still made myself do it. Once I was given a $10 gift by a friend and had spent all but $1.50 of it on food.

When I was at church that Sunday, I felt convicted that I had not given God my tithe on it. As the plate came closer and closer, I began arguing with the Lord.

'You know God that I could use that dollar tithe to buy much needed meat for the family. Surely you wouldn't expect me not to do that?'

Even as I prayed, I felt that still, small voice say, 'Duane, prove me. Just pay your tithe and I will honour you for that.'

So I dropped the dollar bill on the plate, knowing there would be no meat again that week.

Two days later, Ernie Gross, an elder at the little church came around to see us. He was bearing a brown paper bag.

He grinned as he came into the mobile home. 'Hey, I've got 5lb of meat here that I couldn't use, and I want you to have it. Also a whole pile of vegetables,

Could you use them?'

Could we?

'Thank you Lord,' I whispered. 'Once again you have proved faithful if we follow your principle.'

The following day I hobbled down to the mail box before going into my class. There were no letters, but I noticed that there was a pink slip.

I felt a chill in my heart as I fished it out, for I knew that slip spelled trouble.

'You are to report immediately to the Dean of Men's Office,' was the curt handwritten order.

I joined a line of other students who had also received slips. Apparently many had also been absent from the Bible conference without informing the office, while others had unapproved absences.

For what seemed like hours I endured a vigil of waiting propped against the wall with other white-faced students, all wondering what terrible fate would befall them.

Finally, the young man before me came out of the Dean of Men's office shaking his head in anger and shame.

'But you can't ship me,' he shouted indignantly at someone inside the room he had emerged from.

A voice retorted, 'Young man, you are shipped and you will leave the campus immediately!'

I was summoned in. Inside the room were a small solemn-faced group of men from the faculty. They indicated that I should explain why I had this unexcused absence on my record.

'Well that's simple, gentlemen,' I explained confidently. 'I fell from a scaffold and broke my leg. The cast didn't hold so I had to return to the doctor to get it reset and . . .'

'Couldn't you have stopped at the office first and

explained?' interrupted one of the group, lowering his eyes as if burdened with the sight before him.

'No, sir, my leg was so badly swollen that it was an emergency.'

'That's not good enough, Mr Logsdon,' snapped the man who appeared to chair the panel. 'You're shipped!' he added, waving his hand in dismissal.

I looked at him, blinking for a moment, trying to take in the meaning of what he had just said. I was numb with shock.

'I'm shipped ... with a broken leg?' I protested almost plaintively. 'You mean to tell me that after four years of struggling to make ends meet here, and just days away from graduation, you are expelling me?' The words poured out of me with such speed that I retained only a vague impression of what I had said.

'You heard me, didn't you? And that's final. Next....'

I couldn't believe it. Anger and frustration welled up inside me. Surely this grotesque nightmare couldn't befall me so close to graduation. I had coped quite well with my studies and this was the only time I had ever been in any kind of trouble during the whole period.

Fighting back the tears, I pushed the crutches under my arms and went to leave, then I heard a voice to my right say, 'Wait a minute, young man. We're going to make an exception in this case. Mr Logsdon stays.'

Fortunately this professor did have the authority to overrule the man who planned to expel me. He knew that what I had said was true. The tutor had known about the hardships that both Carole and I had endured at Bob Jones. He also knew that Carole had recently been discharged from the university hospital with pneumonia. In fact, he and his wife had been praying for her recovery.

'Thank you, sir,' was all I could mutter as I limped

from the room. The confirmation that all was fine came on May 25th, 1957. I went to my post office box and found a white slip of paper which read, *'???To march or not to march??? From the Registrar of the university, Greetings!'* It continued, 'You have absolutely completed all the requirements for graduation as a result of which you will have your degree conferred next Wednesday. Congratulations! *You are instructed to march.*'

I was overcome with ecstasy. 'It *has* been worth all the struggles,' I whispered to Carole when I later gave her the news. 'It sure has,' she responded.

*     *     *

The Rodeheaver Auditorium was packed to capacity as I stood at the door with some 400 fellow students. We were all proudly waiting to take part in the processional march. The cast had been taken off the previous day and so I could now 'march' with the others. Well, it wasn't exactly a march, more a limp.

My parents had flown in from California for the great event and they joined with Carole in the 3,000-seat auditorium.

My pulse raced as I hobbled down the aisle to a storm of enthusiastic applause to shake hands with Dr Bob who handed me my Bachelor of Arts degree.

'Congratulations for a job well done!' he said as he firmly shook my right hand and gave me the scroll with his left.

A sea of smiling faces greeted all of us as we marched back out of the auditorium. Carole ran into my arms and I was soon surrounded by my sons and my parents.

Feeling very tender and protective about Carole, I

slipped my arm around her shoulder.

'Carole,' I said gently, 'It's been a long march, but with God's help we've come through it. If we can make it through something like this, we can sure finish the course.'

She leaned over and gave me a discreet kiss, laughing and crying at the same time.

'I know we can. Let's set out right now, together on our long march. . . .'

# CHAPTER TWELVE

# Building in a Broken World

'Come on fellas, chop, chop, stop that slacking and let's get that beam moved over to the right side of the foundation.' I stood in my blue overalls 'supervising' the team of volunteers who had been working day and night to help erect a new church in the agricultural community of Idaho Falls.

I pulled a mock, stern face as I continued to scold them. 'Call that work? I reckon a team of old maids could work faster than you lot.'

That was the signal for an impromptu strike, led by Bill Tacklin, a huge mountain of a man.

'Say, Pastor,' he yelled across to me as he made a face of simulated disapproval, 'why don't you stick to preaching, and leave the construction to us?' A round of laughter rang around the room.

I clapped my hands and shouted for a little quiet. 'Look guys, Jesus was a carpenter. He was involved in the construction business, so why can't I follow in his footsteps?'

'Yes,' interrupted Bill, 'but he didn't watch the others work. He got on with the job himself.'

With the kidding over, I joined my friends in the important task of getting the basement enclosed for our new Gethsemane Baptist Church in this community that was beginning to explode after the Atomic Energy Commission had provided new jobs by installing reactors in the nearby desert. This was bringing in hundreds of new families to the area.

I was working with a handful of believers, including some employees of the AEC, in this predominately Mormon town, at assembling a pre-cut church that we had selected from an advertisement in a Christian magazine.

Snow was already beginning to tumble out of the darkened sky as Carole arrived at the site late in the afternoon with the three boys, who began joyfully sliding around outside as Carole inquired how much longer this project was going to take.

'You're never home these days, Duane,' she said, a tinge of sadness in her voice. 'This building seems to be all that matters to you.'

Carole paused for a moment reflecting on the past few months. Then she bit her lip. 'If you'd have taken that church you were offered in North Carolina, you wouldn't be using up so much time putting up a sanctuary.'

Carole shivered as an icy blast of air shot through the site and knifed through her thin coat. Then she added glumly, 'Duane, if you ever get this church finished, you'll probably not even be able to afford pews to go in it. The funds are already fully stretched.'

I had to agree that this site, set in what was once a potato field, was possibly not the most glamorous place to start my ministry as a pastor.

My mind drifted back to when we had stood there a few months earlier during a swirling dust storm and I had remarked to Carole, 'Well, this place doesn't have too many things going for it. But one thing is for sure, we won't be short of spuds.'

Her look told me that she was *not* amused.

I had to agree that if I had accepted the call to pastor

that thriving church in a tobacco farming area of North Carolina, our life would have been much easier materially. I was approached to come and preach 'with a view' while I was still at Bob Jones. I had gone there and was courted by their leaders who felt I was just the young man they needed.

'Preacher,' said one of the elders, his stomach pressed tightly behind a broad leather belt that encircled his pink-coloured trousers, 'if you come here you'll do really well. We'd give you a brand-new car and you could move into the new parsonage we've just built. It's already fully furnished.

'And the sanctuary. Well it's fully air-conditioned. You wouldn't be making a mistake by coming here. We make it a point to take care of our pastor's needs.' The place seemed perfect, yet little questions nagged.

When I discussed the situation later with Carole, I told her that I somehow felt uneasy about accepting the invitation.

'Carole, I really feel that God has called me to be a pioneer and build new churches, not take over those already established.'

Carole took my hand. 'Well, Duane, it's your decision, and I'll back you if you believe God doesn't want you here.' Her serious face blossomed into a smile. 'You know, Duane, one thing has puzzled me about some of the members at this church.'

'What's that?' I said.

She turned her dark eyes on mine. 'Well, they chew tobacco.' We both threw back our heads and laughed at the thought of Christians indulging in what we considered such a strange practice.

I hadn't realized then that Carole didn't feel equipped to be a pastor's wife at *any* church. She found it difficult enough bringing up three bustling boys without the added responsibility of being the wife of an ambitious pastor and having to be the first lady of the church.

Carole later told me, her eyes terribly confused, 'Duane, I felt that when you took your first church that the concert had been planned, the invitations had gone out, and I was to sing, but I didn't have a voice.'

The opening at Idaho Falls had been presented to me by the Pastoral Placement Officer at Bob Jones.

'Mr Logsdon,' he had shared with me in his office, 'there are a handful of believers in a small town in Idaho who are interested in starting a new church there. We've been watching the way you have not only stuck at your studies, but also worked hard at night and on Saturdays to finance your time here. We feel that you could well be excellent material for this kind of pioneering work.'

So I had agreed to route my journey back to Mount Vernon, via Idaho Falls, to meet with the little group. My family dined with Bill and Connie Little, who shared with us their vision for an evangelical witness in the town.

'There is no church in Idaho Falls that stands true to the Word of God,' said Bill, voicing his personal opinion. 'Most of the people around here are Mormons so we would almost be involved in a missionary situation.'

I learned there were two other families in the town, the Porters and the Taylors, who had joined with the Littles in wanting to establish a church.

'Mr Logsdon, there are hundreds of people moving here because of the nuclear reactors, and so we definitely need a positive witness for Christ.'

All that I was hearing was music to my ears. What a challenge this would be! The following Sunday morning, I preached to a small group in a rented building.

That afternoon, I met with the 'Big Three'—Bill Little, Dick Porter and Mansel Taylor—and we discussed the opportunity there was for all of us in Idaho Falls.

'Duane, we can't offer you any income at this time,' said Dick Porter, an atomic physicist who had recently moved into the area. 'But we will make you a promise. If you come, we will work with you one-hundred per cent and support you in prayer and every way we can. What do you say?'

I smiled gently, 'Well, one thing's for sure. If I do come, it won't be for the money. It will be because I believe God is calling me here. If he does, I'll just have to get my plumbing tools out again and earn my bread and butter that way.'

With that, we prayed around in a circle for guidance from God on whether or not I should come, shook hands, and I gathered up my family, and set off towards the Pacific North-West.

*     *     *

Pastor Yaxley scooped up the last drops of a hot fudge sundae, and then fixed his eyes on mine.

'Well, Duane,' he said, as he grabbed a napkin and wiped away traces of the ice cream from his lips, 'you have come to a crossroads in your life. You could go to Idaho Falls, or you could wait for a possible call to an already established work. I know the move to Idaho Falls seems exciting to you . . .' he let the sentence drift to add impact to what he was about to say, 'but remember you will have to work all kinds of hours again to provide for your family. Do you really want to do that? It will be an independent work and you will not have any external support from a denomination. Also it is deep in Mormon country, so you could encounter considerable opposition.'

Pastor Yaxley, as I later discovered, was painting the worst possible picture for me so that if God did call me there, I would have no illusions about what to expect. I would only go because he wanted me there and for no other reason.

'Duane, think all this over and pray about it before you make a final decision.'

That summer flicked away like the pages of a book as I worked hard at the various plumbing jobs that came my way. We were staying at the home of Carole's grandparents.

It wasn't long before I found myself with the Ordination Council of my home church, Emmanuel Baptist. It seemed strange to be seated in front of friends, all wearing serious masks, and firing questions at me relating to theology and doctrine.

'You have to understand, Duane, that this is the rule of the church,' explained Pastor Yaxley, following the mini-inquisition.

After a few minutes' discussion while I was out of the room, he invited me in and shook hands with me.

'Well, brother, you will be delighted to know that we have unanimously agreed that you are ready for the responsibility of becoming a minister. We *will* ordain you!'

The service was set for August 27th, 1957. Deacons of the church called Carole and myself to come to the front so they could lay hands on us both and 'set us apart for the gospel ministry'.

'Lord,' prayed Pastor Yaxley, his voice shaking with emotion, 'please anoint with power these two servants of yours. Give them your strength for the years to come, and help them to remain faithful to you. . . .'

As I opened my dampened eyes, I noticed that Carole's had also taken on a sheen of tears. I squeezed her hand and smiled reassuringly at her.

'I'm sure we'll know soon where we are to go,' I whispered. That night in bed, I was reading my Bible in chapter 33 of Jeremiah. My eyes settled on verse 3: 'Call to me, and I will answer thee, and shew thee great and mighty things, which thou knowest not.' I asked Carole to join me again in asking for clear direction as to where we should go.

Just two days later, Carole came up to me with a letter, beaming all over her face.

'It's got an Idaho Falls postmark,' she said excitedly. 'Let's rip it open.'

I quickly slit the envelope open and discovered inside a letter from Bill Little. I read aloud its contents.

Dear Duane and Carole. After much prayer we as a group feel that you are God's man for Idaho Falls. Although we cannot offer you a salary or even a home at this time, we promise you that as the work begins to grow, we will make it up to you.

Carole then joyfully snatched the letter from my hands and took over the narration!

Please consider this a call to be the first pastor in our new church in Idaho Falls. We will be anxiously awaiting your reply.

I turned to Carole, whose face was now flushed.

'What do you think?' I asked. 'Could this be God's answer to our prayers for guidance?'

She nodded. 'I think you know it is.'

My letter of acceptance was written in a slightly shaky handwriting. I was so overjoyed that this was the place where I would start my ministry that I found it hard to control my excitement.

'Yes,' I penned to Bill Little, 'we will come. God has indicated to Carole and me that Idaho Falls is where we should start our ministry. We'll be there the first week in September.'

*     *     *

Back at that freezing church building site, I looked at Carole, whose nose was turning blue, and observed, 'You know, we've already been here for a year. Yet it seems like only yesterday that we arrived and moved into that dreadful motel.'

There was a slight, uncertain smile on her lips. 'Yes, our friends at the church said we would only have to stay there for two weeks. That two weeks turned into six months!'

I knew that that period had been particularly hard on Carole.

'Duane,' she said sadly, 'that was a time of real loneliness for me. You had your new church to build and your work as a plumber, but I was again the outcast, stuck in a motel this time. Though I guess it wasn't all bad. I had lots of fun with our crazy kids. That experience really threw us together.'

I looked at her, then touched her hand and smiled. 'Well, Carole, I guess it has been a time of building for both of us.'

It certainly had been. I think the biggest lesson I had learned during that time was that I should never ask anyone to do something I wasn't prepared to do myself.

After a few months, the little flock there had been able to start paying me a small salary. That went towards groceries. The money that came in from my plumbing work went towards buying our little house and providing a Christian education for the boys.

One day I said to Carole, 'I believe if we are to get this church finished, I have to set a real example to the others. I have to give sacrificially towards the project.'

Carole looked at me strangely. 'I don't understand you. You already give a 10 per cent tithe and work night and day on the building. What more can you give?'

'Well, I feel I should start giving 20 per cent of my salary from the church back into the building project. If I don't do that, how can I expect the others to give sacrificially.'

So for the whole time at Idaho Falls I doubled the 'legal' tithe, and never once did we go without for our family. God was truly helping me to build for him in a broken world.

# CHAPTER THIRTEEN

# God's Frozen People

I clambered out of bed, cleared the sleep from my eyes and squinted at the clock on my bedside table. Suddenly I remembered what day it was and a warm sensation flooded me.

It was, at last, the *big day*.

I pulled back the curtains. Outside the wind gusted, throwing snow against the windows. Icicles hung wet from our gutters.

'What a day to have our first service in the basement of our new church,' I chuckled.

On hearing my voice, Carole stirred, then pushed herself up on the pillow to a sitting position.

'What's so funny?' she yawned.

'Well, I guess that if that outside thermometer is correct, we could all become *God's Frozen People* at tonight's dedication service. It's a shivering 23° below zero outside.'

Carole smiled gently. 'All I hope is that the heating works tonight.'

The gloom of winter had long since invaded Idaho Falls. But there was no gloom on that Christmas Eve dedication in our temporary subterranean sanctuary. It was full of friends, many of whom had worked very hard on the building of that basement chapel.

As we started the evening of praise and prayer with the singing of the doxology, I glanced around the room. My eyes fixed on Eric Johnson, a slight, crippled man who had provided us with the site for the church. At the back was Bill Tacklun, who had jokingly led a strike all those months back. To my right were Andrew and Olga Titland, the couple who had sacrificed to make the first funds available for the building project.

All were little people in the eyes of the world, believers whose lives apparently had almost no impact outside their own area. But they were typical of many faithful Christians around the world.

'Friends,' I said as I leaned forward and spoke over the top of the podium, 'the birth of Christ was not seen by the masses, yet it made an impact on the world and gave millions a new hope. Although we are just a small group here and few are aware of our dedication service, I predict that the testimony of this church will reach far beyond the borders of this valley.

'Our church is named Gethsemane after the garden where Jesus prayed. Shortly after his time in Gethsemane, the greatest event in history took place.

'So my friends, be prepared for great things in the years ahead. And don't be surprised if we all experience some suffering along the way. After all, this would be a small price to pay for the blessing that will result from what we are doing.'

* * *

I peered down at a group of men crawling around like ants in the dirt under the basement of a house. They were laboriously assembling plumbing fittings in appalling conditions.

I rubbed my chin as Joe Jordan, one of the workmen, came up a ladder from the deep hole.

'That looks like hard work, Joe,' I observed as he wiped his dirt-streaked brow.

'It sure is, Duane. But I guess that's the way we've always plumbed a house, so there's not much we can do about it.'

I paused for a moment. 'I'm not sure that that's true. There has to be a better way.'

He looked puzzled. 'Look, greater brains than yours have tried out a new way to do this and this is still the best they have come up with.'

I suppose when someone tells me that something can't be done I want to prove them wrong.

I had recently been employed as a journeyman plumber by an Idaho Falls firm. My inquiring mind made it difficult for me just to stick to the work I had been allocated.

That night, at home, I got out a sheet of paper and a pencil and began to design a way of pre-assembling all the plumbing fittings on ground level so they then could be lowered as a complete unit in one go. The next morning I took my plan to the boss of the company.

'I reckon this will save you 50 percent of your labour time,' I pointed out to him. 'It will mean that you will be able to double your output each day.'

He looked at me as if I were a space invader.

'How come no one else has ever thought of that before?' he asked.

'I don't know, sir. All I can say is that God gave me an inquiring mind and I have used it.'

The boss extended an exuberant hand for me to grip. 'I think maybe I should give you a little promotion, Mr Logsdon. How about becoming a lead foreman for me?'

I nodded with delight. 'That would be fine. I'd like

that very much.'

* * *

Carole and I stood hand-in-hand admiring the picturesque wooden church that had just been completed. Now, at last, the congregation could meet on ground level instead of in the basement.

'What do you think of it?' I asked her as we stood there alone.

She looked suitably impressed. 'I think it's really fine looking.'

'It hardly seems possible that we've already been here for two-and-a-half years. And now we have a congregation of two hundred, a parsonage, and even a Sunday School bus.'

Carole responded to my enthusiasm. 'Hey, Duane, don't forget the five-minute spot you have on local radio.' My first pastorate was proving to be quite a success.

'You know, Carole, things here seem great, but I've been praying about this and I'm wondering if our work isn't now finished here in Idaho Falls. God seems to be saying to me, "It's time to move on. I've got other fields for you to plough".'

Carole was genuinely shocked at my comments.

'But Duane, won't the people feel abandoned if you left them now?' she asked, a sudden slight edge to her voice. 'After all, you have been through so much together.'

I knew she was right.

'I guess they will, but I'm also sure that if the Lord is leading me out, he has already lined up the person to take my place.'

The congregation was predictably shocked when I

announced that I was moving on. There was a solemn hush as I delivered my farewell sermon.

'When Moses faded from the scene,' I told them, 'God had Joshua standing by in the wings. We've had a great time building this work together, and the Lord has indeed done wonderful things for us in establishing the work in Idaho Falls. I believe it is similar to what he did for the Israelites, when he established them in Canaan.

'Don't be upset that I'm leaving. Let's not look to man, but to God. For the battle is the Lord's.'

There were many tears at the end of the service as we hugged each other and wished each other 'God speed'.

I had arranged that our new home was to be in the palm-studded city of Riverside, in Southern California.

I had already contacted Dr David Schmidt, the regional director of the Independent Fundamental Churches of America. He was based in La Habra, California. Dr Schmidt had wanted to hear a tape of my preaching and, after reviewing it, wrote to me saying there were several churches in Southern California that were in need of a pastor.

'I do not feel you will have any difficulty in finding a pastorate if the Lord is leading you in this direction,' he told me confidently.

I took that as the Lord's will that I should head for California and wait for more direct guidance from there.

While waiting for this direction, I took a job as a plumber with a company in Anaheim, California, where my father was general superintendent. Although it meant a round trip of some seventy miles each day, I was grateful to have work.

Mass-produced housing was now at a peak in Orange County. Tracts were springing up all over the area and I was kept extremely busy installing water pipes to new homes.

I again began trying to work out more sensible ways to instal these lines. The present system was to hang them all from girders and solder them in place.

'Dad,' I said one day as he stood by me at a large site, 'you could eliminate all this labour if you used soft copper and then looped it from fixture to fixture. Then you could solder the manifold together.

'All this could take place on ground level which would make the work easier and certainly more efficient. Then you would instal the complete item at one time.'

Dad gave me the go-ahead to develop my idea and I had soon perfected the method, which meant that I was able to completely plumb four houses a day, instead of the one-and-a-half as before. Soon other plumbers heard of this method and began using it themselves. Now it is in common use all over the United States.

*   *   *

Dr Schmidt had kept me extremely busy on weekends doing what is called 'supply preaching'. That meant that whenever a church was without a pastor, I would fill in for a Sunday.

One day, during a visit to Dr Schmidt, he told me there was a 'fine congregation' in Dunlap Acres, a community near San Bernardino, that needed a pastor.

'Duane, would you like to go out there and supply for them, with the possibility of becoming a candidate as their new pastor?' he asked.

I told Dr Schmidt that I would be delighted to do so. So the following Sunday, Carole, the boys and I drove over to the Community Church of Dunlap Acres, housed in a small building.

As we walked in, I squeezed Carole's hand. 'This church,' I told her, a big smile on my face, 'will need a new building before long, especially if the right man comes along to spark the work.'

She looked doubtfully at me. 'I *hope* you're not getting any wild ideas again.'

'You know me, honey.' She did! Carole knew that inside me was a tremendous drive that caused me to rise to new challenges like this.

After a wonderful morning service with 100 members, they lined up in the aisle to shake hands with me at the door. One elderly gentleman reached out and took my hand. He paused, then spoke softly.

'Mr Logsdon, this really is a great opportunity for the right man. And you might just be that man.'

I thanked him and once again felt the tingle of excitement that always came to me when I knew God was guiding me.

Don, who was now aged nine, had watched what had been going on that morning with interest. As we sped away from the church, he leaned over my shoulder from the back seat, and asked, 'Dad, do you think you might become a preacher here?'

'Well, son,' I said, trying to disguise the excitement in my voice, 'you can never tell what God is going to do.'

Carole looked at me. Her slight smile remained unchanged, 'I think I know you well enough by now to recognize that glint in your eye. It tells me that a move here could be possible. In fact, *more than possible.*'

CHAPTER FOURTEEN

# *'I'm Glad You Left Your Religion at Home'*

Dad looked unusually serious as he spun around in his swivel chair to find me watching him intently.

'Son, I've got a proposition to put to you. How would you like to go into partnership with me in a plumbing business? It's a great opportunity, especially here in Southern California. I've watched you work and I'm convinced that you've got the ability and ambition to make it happen.'

The opportunity my father was offering was very attractive. A building boom was taking place at that time in Orange County and so the profit that we could make would certainly be enormous. Being just part-time in my present work was okay, it helped me make a reasonable provision for my family, but this opportunity could lead to an affluent life for all of us.

'Dad, what you are offering is very tempting, but . . . .' Something inside me had begun to jangle an alarm.

His brow furrowed. 'Son, what "but" can there be?' He rose from his desk. 'You haven't got a church any more, so what's holding you back?'

I reached out and put my hand on my father's. 'Dad, you may not understand this, but God has called me to preach, not run a business.

'I'll work with my hands as long as I need to, but be involved full-time in a business . . . never. That's not my calling.'

Disappointment was written all over his face.

'Well,' he said sadly, 'I suppose you know more about this religion stuff than I do, but I think you're throwing away the chance of a lifetime.'

* * *

The telephone shrilled at our Riverside home.

'It's for you, Duane,' said Carole handing me the receiver. 'Don't be long, or your dinner will get cold.'

I discovered that it was Mr Bert Sudlow, chairman of the board of Dunlap Acres Community Church.

'Mr Logsdon,' the excited voice said over the phone, 'the pulpit committee has asked me to contact you to see if you would be interested in "candidating" as our new pastor.'

My pulse began to race.

'Well, er . . . well, I'll get back to you within a couple of days.'

Over dinner I talked over the situation with Carole.

'Are you really ready to get deeply involved with all the responsibilities of another church?' She was looking at me questioningly. 'After all, this summer has kind of been a holiday for all of us.'

I knew that Carole had hoped to have her 'freedom' a little longer so I said, 'I think I could handle it. But, how about you?'

Her face flushed slightly. 'Duane, you know I have said that I'll follow you wherever you want me to go.' There was a tremor in her voice. 'I want to do whatever God wants me to do.'

Her expression, however, showed me that this was not a move she relished.

* * *

Carole and I sat at the front of the church, our three boys at our side. Looking back I suppose we looked a little like tailor's dummies.

'We are very happy to welcome the Reverend Duane Logsdon, his wife Carole, and his lovely family into our church family.' These words jumped at me from the church bulletin as we waited for our welcoming service, on Sunday, October 4th, 1959, to begin.

'We thank the Lord,' the notice continued, 'for answered prayer in sending them to us.'

We beamed at the congregation who beamed back at us, obviously relieved that they once again had a pastor to help navigate the Dunlap Acres ship.

As at Idaho Falls, I quickly threw myself into my pastoral work. And, as could have been expected, I helped to draw up new building plans for the expansion of the church.

Time slipped by quickly and I had long forgotten about my father's offer to go into partnership with him. I had even forgotten that he had shared with me that he thought there was a possibility that he might lose his job, and felt maybe our partnership could get him out before that happened.

We were just about to begin our evening meal, several months after I had rejected my father's offer, when I heard the noise of a car coming up our drive.

Carole and I went to the window and peeped out. The late afternoon sunshine was slanting down towards dusk.

'Say, isn't that Mum and Dad? But why is Mum driving? Dad is usually at the wheel.'

As they came up the steps of the front porch, I immediately saw something was wrong. Both seemed weighed down with some terrible burden. Their faces were worn and pinched.

'Hi, Mum and Dad,' I said, expecting my mother to reach out and give me the usual hug. It never came.

'Hey, what's wrong? Come on, sit down and tell us about it.'

Dad's face was stamped with pain. 'You tell them, Velma,' he said, shaking his head and sighing hopelessly, 'I don't think I could handle it.'

Mother had a way of coming straight to the point.

'Your father's been fired from his job without notice.' Her voice was high and despairing.

'What happened?'

'There was a shake-up in the company and because your father couldn't endorse some of the new policies they wanted to enforce, he was fired,' she went on forlornly.

'He was told, "If you won't play the game our way, Logsdon, you're fired. Clean out your desk and be gone by five o-clock".' She clenched her teeth and closed her eyes to keep back the tears.

I sat in silence for a moment, praying that God would give me the right words to say at this traumatic time for them both.

'Mum, Dad,' I began uncertainly, 'although men forsake us, God has promised that when we come to him and accept him as our Saviour and Lord, he will never leave us or forsake us.'

Usually, my father would argue with me when I offered one of my sermonettes, but I could see that both he and Mother were now desperately reaching out for help. The lines on his face that had been barely noticeable for so many years had deepened into fissures. I opened my Bible and began to read John 3:16, 'For God so loved the world, that he gave his only begotten Son, that whosoever believeth in him should not perish, but have everlasting life.'

Both of them were looking at me intently.

'I wonder, Dad, if you could have given me up, your only son, and watch me cruelly killed so that others might live. Well, that's what God did through his only Son, Jesus. Wouldn't you like to settle this issue in your lives right now and start a new chapter together with him?'

I waited again for my father's objections, but none came. Instead he said quietly, 'Yes, Duane, it's time.'

Without a moment's hesitation, my parents joined Carole and me as we knelt at the side of the sofa.

I was choking with emotion as I said to them, 'If you both truly want to receive the Lord right now, then repeat this simple prayer after me: "Father, we know that we have fallen short and are sinners and we desperately need your help."' I paused as my mother and father repeated these words after me. '"Please forgive us our sins, come into our lives, pick up the pieces, and help us to walk in your ways for ever. Amen."'

I suddenly burst into tears. They were tears of joy. None of us could contain our feelings, and for several heart-stopping minutes we just allowed the tears to flow freely. I looked at my parents. Their faces had relaxed; expressions of almost undescribable relief flowed across them.

As I dabbed my eyes with a handkerchief, I said, 'Mum and Dad, I've been praying for seventeen years for your salvation. This is a wonderful moment for all of us. Do you realize that bells will be ringing in heaven because of what has happened here today!'

They nodded joyfully.

Then I turned to my father. 'Dad, God can give you back your career bigger and better than you've ever had it before if you will only turn this problem to him.'

He smiled softly. 'Son, after what has just happened, I want to tell you that I believe just that.'

Then his eyes lit up. 'Son,' he said, 'I'm glad you did leave your religion at home this time around. . . .'

# CHAPTER FIFTEEN

# Operation Miracle

Carole's illness seemed never-ending. She spent many hours each day in bed in pain. Her face was pale and drawn, and she could hardly keep down any of the food she ate. Nothing seemed to ease the sickness that wrapped itself around her so tightly.

During the five months of this torment, she constantly asked me desperately, 'When will this end?' We've seen four doctors now and they all seem to have different ideas about what is wrong with me.'

I eased myself onto the side of the bed and held her hand and began mopping her fevered brow with a handkerchief.

'You know, Duane, something's got to be very wrong,' she continued. 'I've lost fifteen pounds since all this began.'

What had confused us both was that Carole had already spent a week in the hospital going through many tests to determine what was wrong with her. But there seemed to be no answer.

The senior doctor had finally decided that Carole needed hormone treatment to deal with her gynaecological illness. She began faithfully taking the prescribed medicine, but still the sickness continued. In fact, she got worse. In desperation I took her to see another doctor I had heard about in Long Beach. He was said to be one of the best of his kind in all of

Southern California.

'Lord,' I prayed desperately in the waiting room as the examination took place, 'please help the doctor find out what is really wrong with Carole right now. I don't think either of us can cope with much more of this.

'Lord, I'm trying to run the church, do my plumbing job, look after the boys and nurse Carole all at the same time. This just can't go on. Please do a miracle and show us what is wrong.'

Just as I completed my prayer, a nurse came out and signalled me to join Carole in the doctor's office. He smiled at me and looked happily at Carole.

'What's he got to be happy about?' I mused angrily.

The doctor's grin continued, 'Well, Mr and Mrs Logsdon, I'm surprised at both of you. Didn't I read in your registration form that you already had three children?'

We nodded in unison.

'Well, you are going to have another.'

He turned to me and I exploded. 'You mean to tell me that Carole's pregnant? She can't be! This hormone treatment she has been taking to make her well again was supposed to have stopped her becoming pregnant.'

The doctor put his hands together patiently.

'Well, Mr Logsdon, I've examined a lot of women and I do have a good idea when one is pregnant.

'But, if you want me to, I can take a test that will definitely prove or disprove whether or not she is going to have another child.'

The tests proved positive, but we went back to see the same doctor with another concern.

'Doctor,' I said agitatedly, 'Carole has been having this special hormone treatment. Do you think it could have any effect on the child she is carrying?'

'Well, it shouldn't, but it *could*.'

As the four months passed before the delivery came, those words kept ringing in my ears. How would we both react if our child was handicapped in any way?

Time dragged on until the moment finally came when I had to take her into maternity at the local hospital.

In the delivery room I held Carole's hand and tried to reassure her that all would be fine. But still we both had a nagging doubt that something could have gone wrong with the baby.

As the contractions came closer and closer together, the doctor came into the room and asked if I would like to watch the birth of my new child. I had never done this before, but I really did want to witness this miracle of birth.

I had to go into another room behind a glass screen while Carole prepared for the big moment. Then suddenly, wonderfully, our son slid out into the world without too much effort. He was picked up by his feet and slapped on his bottom by a nurse, causing him to let out his first cry.

I peered through the window to see if there were any apparent problems with him. But he looked fine. I heaved a sigh of relief.

* * *

That night, Carole was getting agitated. 'Nurse,' she asked, 'why can't I see my baby? Why won't you let me see him? Is there anything wrong?'

The nurse tried to be as soothing as possible.

'Don't worry, dear,' she said, smiling nervously, 'he's having a few eating problems. The doctor will explain it to you in the morning. Now you go off to sleep and have a good rest.'

But how could Carole relax when she knew that something was wrong with her child. She had carried him for nine long months and he had become part of her.

When the doctor came on his rounds the next morning he pulled up a chair beside her bed.

'Mrs Logsdon, your son has a slight problem. He was born with a hole in the soft palate of his mouth, but it is repairable.'

With this Carole burst into tears.

'I know it's all my fault,' she sobbed. 'If I hadn't taken all of that medicine, none of this would have happened.'

The doctor looked stern. 'Now don't go talking like that. This is not your fault. It's just one of those unfortunate things that happen from time to time.

'Now, we are going to bring your son to you and we want to see if you can feed him. It will be quite a problem because of his palate problem. So just be patient and we will help you all we can.'

I would sit with Carole as she desperately tried to feed our little boy, whom we had decided to name Doug. Almost every time she attempted to get him to swallow some liquids he would gag and almost choke.

'Duane, this whole thing is becoming a nightmare for me, I think I'm going to have to let the nurses feed him so I can get some rest,' she said, her eyes full of anguish.

The nurses didn't want Carole to give up in despair, so, for two days, they worked with her at feeding time. But it didn't get any better.

One morning Carole was lying in bed when she saw the doctor fly down the corridor. A nurse then emerged ashen-faced from a side-ward and hissed desperately to him, 'The little boy just took one gasp and was gone.'

I heard him ask, 'Was it the boy with the hole in his mouth?'

Carole strained to hear the reply, but then they disappeared into the room she had just come out of.

'Oh no,' she cried out making a choking sound in her throat, 'my little boy's dead. Oh my God, please help me!'

I was due in a short time to take both Carole and Doug home. Because of a misunderstanding on my part, I was two hours late in arriving at the hospital.

As Carole lay there, her mind a whirl of terrible thoughts, a nurse came over. 'Mrs Logsdon, I want to check your tag.'

She desperately tugged at the nurse's arm. 'Was it Doug that had the problem?'

The nurse did not reply, and vanished from the room. The tears again began to flow from Carole's eyes, and she shook her head hopelessly. She had borne and lost a child within a matter of days. As she rocked back and forth in grief on the bed, the same nurse strode purposefully towards her bearing a little bundle, which she placed in Carole's arms.

'There you are, Mrs Logsdon, here is your little son.'

Carole was stupified. 'But I thought . . .' her voice trailed away. Then she cradled little Doug in her arms, and, for a long moment, just gazed at him. Then she shouted with joy, 'He's alive, oh, thank God, he's alive!'

But that feeling was quickly tempered by terrible tearing sobs, that came from down the corridor. A girl who had given birth on the same day as Carole, had lost her boy. There had been a misunderstanding.

Not knowing anything of this drama, I marched happily into the ward. There was Carole looking flustered as she held Doug tightly.

'Why are you so late, Duane?' she asked, a touch of annoyance in her voice. 'You should have been here three hours ago.'

Then before I could answer, she added, 'Oh, it doesn't matter. What does anything matter? All that I know is that Doug is alive and we're going home.'

*     *     *

'Mum, come quickly, Doug's gone blue again,' shouted Don urgently. Carole and I ran quickly into the bedroom to find our tiny baby slumped backwards, his face now a bluish hue, his body limp.

'Quick,' shouted Carole to me, 'turn him upside down and hit him on the back.' She acted quickly and was able to save his life. But this terrible crisis took place almost every day during the first few months. We were all close to completely cracking up.

We had mounted a twenty-four-hour-a-day vigil between us and other friends and members of the family. But still these emergencies came. There didn't seem to be any end to this situation.

One day, I decided to call a family conference. We gathered in our living room and I explained the situation.

'Look,' I told Carole and the boys, 'the problem is that Doug needs surgery and frankly we can't afford it.' I knew that the operation would cost more than one thousand dollars and on my meagre earnings of eighty dollars a month, there was no way I could pay that sort of money.

I confessed that I had again been trying to solve this

problem in my own strength.

'Yes, Daddy, shouldn't you have prayed instead?' observed Don, a proud grin blossoming, showing how pleased he was that he had taught me a spiritual lesson.

'You're right, son,' I said, ruffling his tousled hair. 'Let's pray right now that God will do a miracle for Doug. Hands up all of you that believe he will answer this prayer.'

The vote was unanimous and my prayer was offered up to heaven.

*　　*　　*

The knock on the front door was firm and insistent. Carole, who had been washing the dishes, wiped her hands on a towel and answered the door.

A smartly dressed young lady stood there.

'Mrs Logsdon?'

Carole nodded.

'Well, let me introduce myself. I'm from the Crippled Children's Service in San Bernardino. I've been told that you have a little son in urgent need of surgery.'

Carole was amazed. 'How did you know about our problem?'

'Let's say that you have a good friend who let us know about your situation. We naturally have to check out your case, but if we are satisfied of your need, we will be able to provide the necessary surgery free of charge for your son.'

The young social worker sat down in a businesslike manner and went over the financial situation and then examined Doug's cleft palate.

'I'll get back to you as soon as I can and let you

know our verdict,' she said.

Just five days later, a call came through from the visitor.

'Mrs Logsdon,' she said with real joy in her voice, 'I'm glad to tell you that you qualify for assistance for your son's medical bills. I am already arranging an appointment for him with one of America's foremost specialists on this problem.'

Carole's hand lingered a few moments on the receiver, then she put it down and called me at the church office.

'Honey,' she said excitedly down the line, 'you know that prayer you gave for a miracle for Doug. Well, it's been answered. Doug's going to be all right at last.'

# CHAPTER SIXTEEN

# 'Pastor, I'm Going to Cut My Wrists'

I was just finishing a hearty breakfast of bacon, eggs and toast, when the phone rang. I wiped my mouth with the back of my hand, and lifted the receiver.

'This is Pastor Logsdon. Can I help you?'

'Pastor, this is Mrs Johnson. Please get over here immediately. If not, I'm going to cut my wrists. I don't want to live any longer. My husband and my children don't love me any more. And . . .'

Her voice was high-pitched, uneven.

'I don't believe God loves me at all.'

I could see that I was going to have to try and get control of this so far one-way conversation.

'Now, Mrs Johnson,' I begged her, modulating my voice to that of a pastor-knows-best tone, 'just calm down and pull yourself together.'

'Now, listen to me,' she cut in, 'I don't want to live any more. Don't you understand that? I want to go home to be with the Lord.'

'Mrs Johnson, suicide is not the answer . . .'

I felt I was botching this whole thing, but I didn't know what to do. Before I could go any further, she interjected again, 'Pastor, you've always said that to be with Jesus is far better. I'm tired of the struggle of everyday life. I just can't go on. You get over here in the next ten minutes, or I'll do it. I'll cut my wrists. I've already got the razor.'

My mind searched desperately for an adequate platitude I could use to calm her down. I knew this lady had a long record of mental illness, but surely there had to be an answer to her problems.

'Look, Mrs Johnson, I agree it will be better to be with Jesus, but in the meantime we've got to allow him to give us the strength to be able to manage the daily pressures that we face. And he has promised to do that.'

'Pastor, I'm going to do it! I'm giving you ten minutes to get here, otherwise I'll be dead and you'll be to blame.'

The line suddenly went dead. Here was a life-and-death situation and I was not even remotely trained to cope with it. I knew very well how to preach a sermon of 'three points and a poem'. I knew how to visit the sick, and conduct weddings and funerals, but I didn't really know how to deal with desperate people.

Carole was out of the house, taking the boys to school, so I dashed to my car and sped out of the drive. The accelerator was pressed to the floor for the one-and-a-half mile drive to Mrs Johnson's home. As my car sped along, I realized what an awesome responsibility that I, as a pastor, had been given.

'Lord, please help me,' I prayed, as my heart raced. 'Give me wisdom and the insight to help Mrs Johnson through this terrible time.'

As I came to their driveway, I saw a white ambulance there. The front door was already wide open. I dashed in and found that Mrs Johnson's husband had overheard the phone call to me and phoned for an ambulance.

Mrs Johnson was lying face down on the bed, sobbing deeply. Two white-coated men were trying to calm her. I placed my arm around her and tried to comfort her.

'But I don't want to go to the hospital,' she sobbed, heavily, and turned on her side. 'I just want to die.'

'Now, now, Mrs Johnson, I'm sure you'll feel better once you get to the hospital.' I mouthed these words, but knew I wasn't getting to the bottom of her deep-rooted feelings of rejection. I really wanted someone else to deal with the situation. It was too complicated for me.

Her face had turned an ashen grey, and her lips faintly blue, which suggested she had already taken a quantity of tablets. Finally, she was persuaded to walk to the ambulance and was driven off to a psychiatric hospital. As I returned home I began praying again, 'Lord, please somehow give me the key to unlock the mystery of dealing with problems like this. I need to be able to meet the needs of desperate people like Mrs Johnson.'

I was met at the porch by an anxious Carole who wondered where I had gone. I explained breathlessly what had happened.

'Mrs Johnson's all right, but not because of my help,' I told her sadly. 'I guess there are lots of people in this world who are really hurting and I don't seem to be able to help them at all.'

Carole looked at me. 'There are lots of people really hurting, Duane. There might even be one in your own family.'

*     *     *

The world suddenly went out of focus as I fell backwards and cracked my head on the concrete floor of Dunlap Acres education building. The temperature had shot up to 120°F and perspiration, for the past hours, had been pouring out of every pore of my body. I was really dehydrated.

I was working with a team of volunteers from the church and we were erecting trusses to be placed in a superstructure that had to hold the roof of the new sanctuary.

Because I was the youngest and most agile of the team, I had volunteered to tie up the rigging, and then climb up the ladder all the way to the top and secure the trusses and untie the rig.

Suddenly, part-way up, I felt my head beginning to spin. I managed to get back down to ground level, then I passed out.

I must have been out for about a minute. When I opened my eyes, I saw one of the ladies of the church leaning over me, wiping my brow with a cold, wet cloth.

'I believe he's had a heat stroke,' I heard one of the men remark. 'He's been overdoing it lately. It seems as if he wants to build the church almost single-handed.'

I was driven home and was able to cool down in a tub of cold water. As I sat there, trying to collect my thoughts, Carole came and talked to me.

'Duane, why is it that the Lord always seems to lead you to a church where you have to do almost everything? Why can't you have a church where you just need to preach?'

She looked at me anxiously. 'Why don't you slow down? This isn't a race, you know.'

How could I tell her that inside me I felt a drive, an urgency to complete projects. It was as if I needed mountains to climb.

After a few days of letting my body get strong again, I heard that some of the church members had proposed that I get a salary increase. A member of the church told us later that there had been one dissenting voice. A deacon had stood up at the church meeting and said, 'Let's not be too liberal. My philosophy is that if you keep them hungry, you keep them humble.'

I was upset when I heard this, but I told Carole, 'Well, I suppose God did call us here for better or for worse.'

We did get that small rise and within a few weeks many people had rallied round to complete the new church building. But even as the church was dedicated, I began to get itchy feet again.

That night, Carole snuggled up to me in bed.

'Duane, I watched you at the service today. You looked so happy, but I can read you like a book. I know it will only be a matter of time before we move on. Am I right?'

I nodded.

'I guess I'm a church-builder. That's what I'm called to do. I then need to let someone else take over.'

*     *     *

'Come on boys, it's time to get up and get at it. It's five-thirty on the button.' I went from bedroom to bedroom shaking the three oldest boys.

'Oh Dad,' protested Danny, now aged eight, 'can't we sleep for a few more minutes?'

'No,' I said firmly. 'We have to work our hour and then Mum will have breakfast for us.'

David now also began to protest. 'But Dad, why do we have to get up so early every morning and work like this? The other kids at school don't have to do this.'

'Because, son, we must work together to provide for our family needs.'

'But why can't the church pay you enough to live on, like other pastors?' he wailed.

We had moved to another pioneer work in the city of Redlands, which was some five miles away from Dunlap Acres, and had an unusual claim to fame. Redlands had the first line painted down the middle of the street to keep traffic orderly. I had been approached by a representative of some seventeen families there who wished to form the nucleus of a new church.

'Well, David,' I said, answering his question, 'they will, once the church is built up. This is only temporary.'

The three boys reluctantly got up and went to the bathroom to wash the sleep from their eyes. I led them in the darkness to the carport where I switched on the lights and we got down to business.

'Okay boys, now be careful with those belt-sanders. One mistake and they could take all the skin off your fingers.'

Within minutes they were all doing their allotted tasks.

'Ouch,' yelled Doug as he dropped a piece of copper tubing and watched in horror as a blister began to form on the tip of his thumb and first finger of his right hand.

'Son,' I told him, 'you've got to learn that hot copper can be dangerous if you don't handle it properly.'

'Now you tell me,' he wailed as he hopped up and down in pain.

After sixty productive minutes Carole called from the kitchen. 'Breakfast's ready. Work's over for the day.'

There was a cheer and then a mad rush to the kitchen, which meant I had to clear up the mess myself.

'I don't know, you guys are something else,' laughed Carole. 'You certainly haven't inherited your dad's love for hard work. Never mind, you're learning something that is worth while.'

'What's that, Mum?' they chorused.

'You're learning that you don't get anything for nothing in this life.'

Dan looked at Carole. 'That's not what Dad preached about on Sunday. He said that God's gift of salvation is free. You don't have to work for it.'

Carole laughed. 'Well that is true. But it still doesn't mean you are going to get out of more work tomorrow.'

I had realized something new about tithing while at Redlands. It occurred to me that this didn't just involve the giving of money, but also of time and talent. And so I poured my time and talent into the building programme there. And I only took a minimal salary so that most of the money given to the church could go towards the sanctuary, hymn books, Bibles and musical instruments.

Even during this time, God honoured this action. Besides the work I was doing for my father, I also got a one-day-a-week contract to repair leaking taps in the area. I would travel around with Carole typing up the bills in the car on a portable typewriter. Usually we would get about $150 for that one day's work each week. More than enough for our needs.

Coming back after a good Monday's work, I remarked to Carole in the car, 'The more I see of God's hand in all this, the more I marvel. It certainly is true that if you sow sparingly, you will also reap sparingly.'

Carole joined in. 'And if you sow bountifully, you

will reap bountifully.'

Her eyes were now alight. 'Anyway, we're not giving up anything, Duane, it's all his in the first place.'

# CHAPTER SEVENTEEN

# 'Are You Through Yet?'

Carole put her face in her hands and began to weep uncontrollably. The doctor leaned over his desk and handed her a box of tissues.

'Mrs Logsdon,' he said with just a trace of annoyance in his voice, 'stay as long as you like—until you get control of yourself. Use the whole box if you want to.'

With that he scurried out of his office to another appointment. Carole was really unwell this time. She was suffering from terrible migraine headaches, abdominal pains and bouts of dizziness.

She had just spent twelve days in the hospital for tests and the doctor had given his verdict.

'Mrs Logsdon, it seems to me that you are a border line diabetic. However, you could control this with a diet. There's nothing else physically wrong with you that would cause the symptoms you have been having.

'You've told me that you are a Christian. Maybe our resident psychiatrist could try and separate some of the emotional problems from those you think are of a spiritual nature.'

Those remarks were like a knife into her soul and set her off crying again. Carole had always believed that the Lord could help solve all physical and emotional situations. The thought of being emotionally unstable not only reflected badly on her, but was also a slap in the face of God. Carole believed that Christians should not have emotional problems.

She told me later that she felt a total failure as a Christian, a wife and a mother.

As the tears coursed down her cheeks and Carole tried to stem the flood of pent-up frustrations with her tissues, a nurse pushed open the door.

'Are you through yet?' she snapped sourly.

That caused Carole to cry even more.

'We are going to need this room in a couple of minutes, so why don't you take the box of tissues with you and go somewhere else?'

When I arrived in the waiting room to pick Carole up, I could see from the pink rims around her eyes and the dark circles under them that things were still bad.

She fell into my arms. 'Duane, I'm so low I can't tell you. I feel the Lord has failed me. I don't know if there is any answer.' Her black depressions wrapped around her like a chain and nothing seemed to ease its stranglehold upon her.

I was totally bewildered by my wife. For long periods she would be extremely ill and depressed, and I did not seem to be able to comfort her, or even reach her. Life for both of us had become an impenetrable fog.

As we drove home, Carole looked at me, desperation in her eyes. 'I know this must seem like the seventh verse of the same song, but I can't help it. I don't want to feel like this, but *I just do*.' She shook her head and sighed hopelessly.

When we got home, Carole immediately headed for the bedroom and lay listlessly on top of the bed, staring up at the ceiling, listening to the sounds of silence. She did this hour after hour for many days.

After I went to the church office, Carole would get

up briefly, take a shower, put on a clean nightdress and go straight back to bed.

One day I went up to Big Bear Mountain to work with my father on a cabin he was building. We were caught in a terrible snowstorm and had a nightmare journey home.

The wipers on my car had struggled back and forth vainly trying to clear the snow from the windscreen as we slid all over the road. I arrived home three hours later than I had planned, grateful that I was still alive.

As I opened the door, Carole blew up.

'Well, you might have rung! I've been worried sick.' With that she burst into tears.

I couldn't cope with that sort of behaviour and snapped back, 'Well I'm just thankful that I am still alive. I'll talk to you later when you are more rational.'

I went straight into our bedroom and fell into bed. Almost immediately I sank into a deep sleep. After a few hours I awoke to see Carole's silhouette pacing the floor, her head in her hands.

'Darling,' I said as I slipped away the covers and went over to her, 'What's wrong?' I put my arm around her and tried to comfort her.

'Duane, I can't go on. I feel something terrible is about to happen.'

'Come on, Carole. Let's go back to bed. A good night's sleep will help us all feel better.' Cradled in my arms, she finally fell off to sleep.

When the alarm went for Carole to get up and pre-pare breakfast for the kids, I jumped up. She was in a deep sleep and certainly not in any shape to do any housework.

The boys were as lively as ever as I provided them with cereals and milk. When they left, I sat down on the settee and began to reflect on what was happening in my marriage. I realized how isolated we had become from each other.

'Lord,' I cried out, 'what can all this mean? I'm trying to serve you, but all the time Carole is ill. How can I minister to others, if I can't even help my own wife?'

'Is this a test of faith or a message from you? Have we been disobedient in something? I just don't understand why we are going through this.'

I allowed my mind to run wild. Everywhere I had gone, the church had grown rapidly and we saw great blessings. Yet at the back of this, my wife would soon begin to crumble both physically and emotionally under the pressures and responsibilities of being a pastor's wife. On the business side too, I was seeing success. My little inventions were now proving successful and I had begun patenting some of them. That sideline was growing and without much effort from me. But what was the point of all of this if my marriage was a mess?

'Lord, this whole nightmare is a puzzle to me,' I continued in my anguished talk with God. 'Is it the ministry that is making Carole ill, or are you using her illness to lead me out of it?'

'Please give me the wisdom to unravel this puzzle. In fact, Lord, don't lead me, *push me*!'

He did! We finally discovered that Carole had a serious internal problem and surgery became necessary. This was partly the reason for her feeling so low. She began to perk up again after her operation. For a time....

* * *

Carole had started going out again with me and the boys. One evening we had decided to go to a nearby coffee shop for a treat.

'When are we going to eat?' complained Doug. 'I'm absolutely starving.'

At that moment, a waitress sailed by, laden with a plateful of buttered toast for another customer. He snatched a piece as deftly as one of Fagin's little band of thieves in Victorian London, and began devouring it. Unfortunately for him, the waitress had spotted his action, put down the plate on our table and slapped his hand.

Doug was so humiliated that he began to cry.

'I'm sorry, love,' said the embarrassed waitress. 'But you can't go around stealing other people's things.'

Carole agreed.

'You're right, miss, he had it coming to him.'

As this drama unfolded, I was deep in my doodling. (When an idea came to me, I would get out my pen and begin designing a new product on a paper napkin.) Carole saw me at it again and exploded, 'Why can't we just go out and have a meal without you spending half your time with doodles?'

I smiled.

'I won't be long this time. I think I've got it. Look can you see what I am doing? I'm designing a tub box that will accommodate waste water underneath a bathtub.'

Carole leaned over and took my arm. 'Duane Logsdon,' she said, smiling weakly, 'you're too much.'

I was pleased to see Carole was beginning to emerge from her nightmare. Because of the success of my little business partnership with my father, Carole had agreed to help in the office. And she was doing a great job, taking orders and generally making sure that the paper work was taken care of.

'You know, Duane,' she bubbled one day, 'I really

enjoy working here. It's much more enjoyable than being a pastor's wife—and much easier.'

# CHAPTER EIGHTEEN

# Specialty Products

'Duane, how do you keep coming up with these new ideas?' asked Joe Johnson, a businessman interested in my products, as he lit up a cigarette and breathed the harsh smoke into his lungs.

I was in a restaurant in Anaheim with Joe, the chief executive of a large plastic plumbing-producing company based on the West Coast. He had sat there open-mouthed as I had described some of my inventions.

'You can see, Joe, that all of them are specialty products for the plumbing trade. That's why we've called the company "Specialty Products".'

'Sure, sure, Duane,' he said impatiently, his brow wrinkling, 'but you haven't answered my question.'

I wasn't sure whether Joe realized that I was a pastor. I had recently decided to leave Redlands and concentrate for a while on the business and then see what the Lord had in mind for me. But still, I knew I should use the moment to witness to him.

'Joe, I really believe God gives them to me.'

'Are you kidding?' His eyes grew large with frank curiosity. 'You mean to say that God actually gives you the design each time?'

I began to explain to Joe that I believed that we were, as the Bible said, 'fearfully and wonderfully made'.

He sat in silence watching me thoughtfully as I continued, 'That means that we are all made individuals and given our talent and ability, as well as personality, to perform a certain job or role in life.

'I believe that he put me here to use my abilities to create things to be used for him.'

I could see that he was still confused, so I went on. 'Well, you see Joe, first of all I'm a Christian. That means I've accepted the Lord Jesus Christ into my life as my personal Saviour. I have an assurance that my sins are forgiven and can look forward to eternal life. Because he has done that for me, I want my life to be fruitful and an honour to him.'

Joe stubbed out his cigarette into the ashtray in front of him and thanked me for my sermonette. He then turned the conversation to how these products could be manufactured.

At the end of the lunch, he shook my hand warmly.

'Duane, it's been a pleasure. Thanks for sharing your faith with me. I'm not saying I'm completely convinced, but you've sure got me thinking.

'And incidentally,' he added as an afterthought, 'I hope your inventions make you a lot of money.'

His good wishes were soon turning into a reality. It seemed that whatever I invented was quickly adopted within the trade, and sales for the product were almost immediate.

*     *     *

Carole looked radiant at her desk in our new office.

After greeting me with a kiss she said, 'We are getting orders from as far away as Chicago, Dallas and Philadelphia. It's really exciting. I know that was a big thing for you to leave Redlands, but I also know that God is blessing this business. And I feel better than I have for years.'

We had not had a real holiday together for a long time, and I thought it would be nice if we could combine business with pleasure by attending a trade convention in Hawaii. I knew we needed more representatives for our products, and this was the ideal place to make contact with them.

Carole was ecstatic with the thought.

'Oh, Duane, do you really mean it? I've always dreamed of going to Hawaii.'

The wheels of the Boeing 747 struck the ground at Honolulu and the plane screamed along the runway. As it braked, we both felt we had landed in paradise. Hawaii was everything we had imagined it to be, with sun-drenched beaches, swaying palm trees and beautiful people.

The convention proved a huge success, and I was able to add considerably to our sales force. When we arrived back at Los Angeles International Airport, we were delighted to be met by Bonnie Morris, my sales secretary, her husband Guy the National Sales Manager at that time, and our son Dave and his wife.

As we walked throught to the luggage area I noticed them carrying a huge banner which read, '*Welcome Home. We hit $100,000 plus this month!*'

Carole jumped up and down with excitement. 'Isn't it wonderful?' said Carole. 'God is really blessing the business.'

I held her tightly as the others milled around.

'It is wonderful,' I said uncertainly. 'But I can't understand it. Why is God blessing us? We really don't deserve it.'

* * *

The chimes of the front doorbell echoed around the house. I opened the door to be confronted with a kind-faced man.

'Mr Logsdon?' he inquired. 'My name is Dee Johnson. I'm the chairman of the pulpit committee of Anaheim Community Church. I understand you might be available for pulpit supply. We've been without a pastor for some time and I wondered if you would like to come and preach for us this Sunday?'

I invited Mr Johnson in and was strangely warmed by his friendly manner. As we sipped coffee, he explained that the church had been without a pastor for two years.

'We are trusting that the Lord will send us his man very soon,' he added.

I said I would be delighted to preach, and that Sunday I spoke at two services, both of which had about 175 people. I was warmly received by all.

The following week, Dee Johnson called me and said that everyone had enjoyed my ministry and would like me back again. So I was soon back in the pulpit.

I deeply loved ministering God's word and began to wonder why my business commitments seemed to be side-tracking me from my first call—to be a pastor.

At the close of the second service, Mr Johnson called me into the pastor's study with a proposition.

'Duane, is there a possibility that you might be interested in being a candidate for pastor of this church?' he asked directly.

I paused for a moment. I found the possibility extremely attractive. But how could I fit in more work? In addition to the business, I was taking a master of arts degree and my thesis was to be on pioneering churches.

'Dee, I am really flattered that you should ask, but under the present circumstances, I can't see how it could be done. However, thanks for considering me.'

I shared this with Carole as we drove home from the church.

'So what was your reply, Duane? Did you accept?'

'No, I didn't. I told him that it would be an impossibility at this time.' A wry smile crossed Carole's face.

*    *    *

I soon discovered that Dee Johnson didn't give up that easily. Week after week he would invite me to preach at the church, and week after week I would accept. Then one day he asked me if I would meet with five of the church leaders as they wanted me to tell them about my philosophy of running a church.

'But why do they want me to do that? That should come from the person who is candidating for pastor,' I protested to Dee.

'Well,' he said, avoiding my question, 'why don't you just come along and see? Maybe we can all learn something.'

I shook hands with the deacons who asked a number of questions about my views on different aspects of the leadership of a church. It was all very interesting, but I couldn't quite see the point.

Then I did!

'Mr Logsdon,' said one of the deacons, 'you seem admirably suited for the position of pastor of Anaheim Community Church. Is there any way you would consider yourself a candidate? I mean, any way?'

I again went through my present responsibilities and said I thought it would be difficult, if not impossible to carry another load, especially one so time-consuming.

'Look gentlemen, I'll make you a promise. I'll pray about the situation.'

I shared their request with Carole and I could see that she was not one hundred per cent sold on my becoming a pastor again.

'Duane,' she said, 'I want to tell you one thing. If God does show you that he wants you to be the pastor there, I'll back you.' But I could see from the cloud of concern in her face, that she was not looking forward to this.

Then her face lit up. 'Well, one thing's good about this. At least this church is already built. You wouldn't have to go through one of those awful building programmes again!'

# CHAPTER NINETEEN

# The Missing Circle

At my office in the Anaheim Community Church, I always seemed to be counselling someone with an "insurmountable" problem. I had finally accepted the invitation to become pastor of this already well-established body of believers and was about a year into my pastorate. One morning while leafing through my mail, I came across a brochure from the Narramore Christian Foundation offering a three-week seminar for missionaries and pastors, and their partners.

'Wow,' I exclaimed to Carole over lunch, 'this is just what I need. These days I can only help a few of those who want counselling from me. I feel so inadequate when they bring me their never-ending problems. This course is supposed to equip us so-called professionals to deal more effectively with human relationships.'

So both Carole and I enrolled for their March 1975 course at the beautiful Narramore headquarters in Rosemead, California, to be conducted by Dr Clyde Narramore. This highly respected man had served for thirteen years as a consulting psychologist on the staff of the Los Angeles County Superintendent of Schools, and later developed an international counselling and training ministry in Southern California.

When the course began, we both sat listening intently to Dr Narramore, as he led an orientation session:

'When you consider your attitudes, the way you look at things, your feelings and your behaviour, you might ask yourself, "How did I get this way?" "Why do I act the way I do . . . and why do other people act the way they do?"

'Let's look at a basic principle. All behaviour is caused. There's always a reason why people act as they do. Furthermore, causes are multiple. Several dynamics go together to produce a certain behaviour.'

He would later look at these dynamics. The psychologist then observed that recent advances in knowledge, world conditions and family problems had put terrible pressures on many people today and 'mercilessly ground them under the so-called wheels of progress.'

He continued: 'From every corner of the world come cries for help. The depressed mother in Europe, the bewildered boy in Africa, the tormented adolescent in the Orient, and the deviant father in America, all plead for better adjustment.

'As important as each profession may be, none offers greater challenge than the field of human understanding, especially on an individual basis. The counsellor who sits face-to-face with a disturbed person is challenged by the important question: "How can I help someone to be a well-adjusted human being, so that he can function adequately during his years on earth?"'

I found all this most interesting. I wanted to help people become well-adjusted. It was fascinating material.

'To say,' continued Dr Narramore, 'that the human organism is complex would be an understatement. God's eternal word eloquently describes man when it declares in Psalm 139:14—"I will praise thee; for I am fearfully and wonderfully made: marvellous are thy works; and that my soul knoweth right well." Thus, the man who is called upon to counsel is in great need of wisdom. Nothing is more intricate and complex than humankind.'

Dr Narramore declared that a counsellor needed to be the kind of person who was an example of excellent integration and adjustment. Was I really like that? I began to ask myself.

The doctor explained that there were three large circles which represented the basic causes of human behaviour. They were physical, spiritual and emotional.

'Each of these impinges upon the other. Although they are somewhat discrete, they continually affect one another,' he added.

Dr Narramore then looked around the room which contained about eighty people, many of them married couples, and said, 'By the end of this seminar you will be given life-changing keys. You are not here to be lectured to . . . you are here to be changed. By the end of three weeks, I believe you will experience a real change. We will begin by diagnosing your needs.'

He put a diagram on the blackboard:

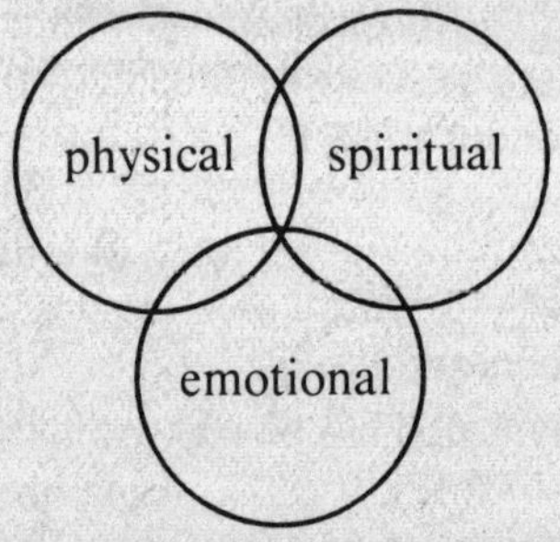


Then he gave examples of physical problems and

how they influenced our thinking about ourselves, others, God, the Bible, and almost everything.

Next he explained the spiritual circle: human beings are spiritual beings; they have spiritual needs that demand spiritual solutions. I agreed quite readily to that one.

Then he dealt with the emotional circle. His treatment of the emotional causes of behaviour was really outstanding but rather painful.

'I'm going to ask you to do two things: first, be open and honest about your feelings. Don't tell me how the Bible says you *should* feel. I already know that. Instead, tell me how you really *do* feel deep down inside. Secondly, force yourself to talk. Few insights and changes will come until you talk.'

*　　*　　*

'I didn't come here to be analysed by a shrink,' I fumed to Carole, during the morning break. 'Look, Carole, I don't know what's going on here, but I thought I was just going to develop some skills to help other people. Now why are they turning this on us?'

Up to then, I had enjoyed every minute of the seminar. But when it was announced that we would all be given several psychological tests, I didn't like that at all. That meant I would have to reveal, to someone I didn't know, my innermost feelings and thoughts.

'Well, Duane, it's too late to back out now,' Carole answered, trying to soothe me. 'Let's just take the tests and see what comes out of it.'

I couldn't believe what we were asked to go through. One test required me to draw a house. Afterwards, I again fumed to Carole, 'Well, that was completely ridiculous. Fancy asking us to draw that. Do they think this is a play school?'

Then they gave us the other tests, some long, some short. I was still angry when I met a counsellor who was to interpret the results of our tests. He looked at my test scores, then my drawing of a box-like home. After clearing his throat, he said, 'Well, Mr Logsdon, I see you have quite small windows on your house. That's usually an indication that a person does not want another person knowing much about his personal life.'

I felt a slight burning sensation at the back of my neck. I was floored, for I knew that was true. Then he pointed out many other things. The more he spoke, the more uncomfortable I felt. He was telling me that I needed to be more open and honest in my life. But I knew that being honest, especially with one's flock, was a great risk. People at church expected the pastor to be an example, not a fallible human being like them.

Carole had her appointment with the psychologist. Then it was her turn to walk ashen-faced from her test interpretation session. She was even more shaken than I was.

'Duane,' she said, her lips trembling, 'I felt uneasy the whole time the counsellor was talking to me. I discovered there are reactions in my life that are not glorifying to God.

'Boy, it's really hard to look at yourself with the wrappers off!'

I had to agree.

'Carole,' I said, clasping my wife's hand, which was warm with nervous perspiration, 'I guess in our marriage we've done an awful lot of talking, but very little communicating.'

*　　*　　*

Hour after hour, day after day, Carole and I sat side-by-side experiencing dull pain in our hearts.

We had sessions throughout the day . . . even some in the evening. Dr Narramore spoke many times. He also introduced other remarkable psychologists, all Christians, who spoke to us and reasoned with us. They all knew what they were saying. I was really impressed . . . but uncomfortable. We were all living on campus, so we couldn't very well get away.

Possibly for the first time in our married lives, we had begun to gain insights into what made us tick and why we acted as we did. We both felt physically and emotionally drained, as these different probes stripped away the defensive layers in our minds.

'The secret is understanding yourself,' explained one of the speakers. 'Don't expect perfection, but do expect progress. Not idealism, but identity. Don't expect to arrive in one go, but you do need to experience the maturing process.'

After one session, which again had set us back on our heels, we reflected on what Dr Narramore had said at that first session about the three circles.

Carole told me in our room, 'I've begun to realize that there is one entire circle missing in my life. I exist in the spiritual and physical, but the emotional is almost annihilated.

'Maybe we've really come here because we need insights into our own lives before we can ever help others.'

It was strange, but whenever the teacher made a statement that was general, I felt fine, but when he became personal, I felt angry again.

Near the end of the three weeks, one of the counsellors related the story of a husband-and-wife conflict. He then asked each person in the room to comment on how we interpreted the incident.

He turned to a senior pastor sitting close to Carole and me and said, 'How do you feel about that, Joe?'

'Well,' he responded with all the confidence of a well-educated Christian leader, 'I think if she had done what he had asked her to do, they would not have arrived at that point of tension in their relationship.'

The counsellor tried to be patient. 'Yes, Joe, but how do *you* feel about it?'

'Well,' replied Joe his voice rising, in exasperation, 'I still believe that if she had done what. . . .'

Just as he was getting more wound up, the counsellor cut in. 'Excuse me, Joe, but I asked how *you* felt about the incident.'

Not only Joe, but all of us realized that here we were, supposedly professionals with training at Bible schools, seminaries or colleges, influencing people and dealing with their lives, yet we seemed to be totally out of touch with how people really felt. This was a shattering revelation.

As the excrutiating process continued, I wondered how much more we could take.

Soon I had to agree with Carole that the irony of the whole situation was that we had come to learn how to help others better, but we were having to learn how to help ourselves first.

As we sat there listening to these godly, skilled psychologists, it began to dawn on us both that neither of us had a totally rounded personality, and that that needed to be remedied.

The initial taking-to-pieces process was painful. Wrappers were being torn away as counsellors got right down inside us. Night after night Carole and I talked into the early hours like we had never done before. Then we would kneel and pray together, confessing to God our innermost problems.

'Don't give up,' said one of the leaders during a particularly tough time for all of us. 'Realize that everyone has these kinds of problems. And there is a way out.'

He explained that we really needed to understand ourselves by being willing to identify our weaknesses, faults and frustrations, then discuss them openly with our partners or friends, and accept the responsibility of change.

'You know, Duane, I never thought I could share with you how I have felt all these years,' Carole said that evening, her voice faltering slightly. 'I find it frightening and exciting. I suppose I never wanted you to know how I really felt about myself in case you left me. I feel I've been such a horrible person.'

I held Carole close. 'You're not a horrible person. I'm the one who has never understood what you have been going through.'

As we just held each other tight, Carole said through a sheen of tears, 'Thank you for putting up with me all these years.'

What could I say? 'Carole, a floodgate has been opened in our lives and our marriage. Never again must we let it close. We've got to keep the lines of communication open.' I loosened my hold of my wife and then gave her a long, loving look.

We began to talk over the way we had brought up our four sons. I felt guilty that I had often been too busy to spend much time with them, and Carole felt that her constant illnesses had caused her not to be as patient and understanding with them as she should have been. In a sense, they had been emotionally deprived.

One by one we called our boys at their homes and

apologized for being poor parents. It was a time of much tears and emotion for us all.

David's response was typical. 'Look, we don't think you've done such a bad job. We weren't so perfect ourselves.'

During the three-week seminar we had been diagnosed. We faced the diagnosis and accepted it. We had brought feelings and attitudes out where they could be handled . . . and we dealt with them. Through tests, counselling, discussions, plus the application of God's word, we had gone through the process of change.

On the final night, Carole and I opened our Bibles and began sharing verses with each other that had taken on a new meaning for us. Carole turned to Psalm 40, verse 3, and read: 'And he hath put a new song in my mouth, even praise unto our God: many shall see it, and fear, and shall trust in the Lord.'

Her face relaxed, and an expression of almost indescribable relief flowed across it.

Finally she said happily, 'Because of these three weeks, I really believe that God has given me a new song.'

# CHAPTER TWENTY

# 'Lord, Help This Silly Business Go Broke'

The Narramore experience was so vital and life-changing that our marriage was transformed. It gave us a new lease on life. We became total lovers, friends, parents, really for the first time.

At last we were pulling *for* each other, instead of against. Knowing Carole's dislike of being the 'first lady' of a church, I was delighted one day as we were driving to the morning service and she said, her eyes sparkling, 'You know, I think it's really great being a pastor's wife.'

I never thought I'd ever hear Carole say that.

She was now bubbling with excitement. 'Well, I learned so much at the seminar that I am beginning to understand what makes me tick,' she exclaimed. 'God gave me so many answers that I feel I want to share them with other people out there who are in distress.'

It wasn't long before Carole discovered a course on wives' relationships with husbands and began teaching it at the church. I just couldn't believe what had happened to both of us. Each day was a joy. No longer did we go through the motions of prayer and Bible reading. Now it was vital, alive, real. It was I who now had to quicken my pace to keep up with her.

Carole supported me in my pastoral duties in a way she had never done before. At last she felt a total woman. She was even asked by Dr Narramore to be one of the first speakers at his national Personal Enrichment courses.

'I want to share with you the hang-ups, both spiritual and emotional, that hindered my relationship with my husband, my family and the people around me,' she began her first talk.

I would sit in an audience and beam with pride as Carole became a speaker much in demand. She was vivacious, witty and powerful in her presentation. It was because she had lived through what she was teaching.

Then she began training as a medical assistant, taking a nine-month course. When Carole was in Mount Vernon, at school, she was a C student, but now she came through the classes with an A average.

After that course, she did an internship with a local doctor for three months, and then enrolled in a nearby college for courses in psychology and social studies.

Carole's whole appearance had changed. She began to take special care of her appearance and was constantly bubbling over with enthusiasm.

'You know, Duane,' she shared with me before we began our evening devotions together, 'I feel I don't even want to sleep at night in case I miss anything that God has for me. And before, I didn't even want to get up out of bed.' I smiled, remembering vividly those nightmare days.

As we had now vowed to tell each other everything, I asked Carole to listen to what I had to say.

'I have never told you this before, but shortly before we went to the seminar, I went to see a doctor about you. He knew all about your case and told me that I had some big decisions to make. He told me that my job as a pastor, the pressures of the parsonage, plus the other pressures of being a business executive's wife, were possibly more than you could handle. He said that if I made the wrong decision about what I did with my life, I could push you right over the edge.'

Carole listened intently, a slight, uncertain smile on her face.

'Thanks for telling me that, Duane. Now may I share something with you? I've always wondered why we could not grow together spiritually at the same pace. You always seemed miles down the road from me and I suppose I did get very bitter with God at times.

'I've always felt hurt that I was not of more help to you and couldn't understand what you were up to most of the time. I suppose there was a real communications barrier between us. You were in your small corner, and I was in mine.'

She paused for a moment to wipe a tiny tear that had appeared in her eye.

'I'm beginning to realize for the first time the incredible pressure you have felt in building up a growing church and also running a corporation that was getting more successful by the day. I can see, Duane, that you are in a really impossible situation. I think that soon you are going to have to make a decision about which comes first, the business or the ministry.'

*　　*　　*

We had, by now, five full-timers on the staff at the church, and Specialty Products had grown to be a nationally recognized plumbing specialty company. We had offices on the East Coast of the United States, as well as the West. We had a catalogue of one-hundred-and-fifty items, and had recently moved into a thirty-five thousand square foot building, close to

Anaheim. At that time, in 1975, our turnover was nearing five million dollars per year and had been doubling each year.

I found myself being stretched incredibly between running the church and also the business. I became worried that I couldn't really do my pastoral work properly with the business growing at the pace it was. So I would call for regular meetings with the church board asking them for an evaluation of my ministry.

'Gentlemen,' I told them one night, 'I want each of you to take off the gloves and share your honest feelings with me.'

One by one they gave me a vote of confidence. They pointed to the fact that the church was nicely filled each Sunday, people were committing their lives to Christ, the youth and missionary support programmes had grown dramatically.

The votes of confidence that I kept getting from the board made it very difficult for me to open up myself to what God really wanted me to do. The last thing I wanted was to hurt these dear friends of mine.

Carole was also enjoying her new life in the church. In a dramatic reversal of roles, she had even begun to pray, 'Lord, help this silly business go broke. I know the ministry is Duane's first love and calling, and I want him to stay in that.'

Much to Carole's chagrin, I really did enjoy my life in the business world. Gifts like that of administration, which I hadn't realized I had, were being used fully in that sphere.

Soon I faced another, rather unusual problem. A surplus of money. The royalties from my various patents had begun to pay handsome dividends and thousands of dollars were pouring in. This also meant, however, that I was having to pay very high taxes on the money.

'Surely,' I told Carole, 'there must be something I could do about this situation. I wonder if the Lord is trying to tell me something.'

* * *

We were both beginning to get very exhausted with our hectic non-stop lives. So I suggested that we get away for a short break.

'Carole, I understand there's going to be a conference in Bellingham, Washington, close to Mount Vernon, at a place called "The Firs". It is organized by Overseas Crusades. Why don't we go there?'

'Sounds good,' murmured Carole. 'And we could look in on Mount Vernon and see some of our old friends.'

I really enjoyed the ministry at this challenging conference, but I was taken into another dimension when a dynamic Argentinian-born evangelist, Luis Palau, began to speak.

'Brothers and sisters,' he enthused in his winsome way, near the end of his talk, 'I believe that we will have preached the gospel to all the Spanish-speaking people of the world by 1983.'

'Will you stand with us as we do this?'

I have never seen anyone preach like this evangelist. His presentation was fresh, exciting and thoroughly annointed by God.

As I had been drawn more and more into the sermon that Mr Palau was preaching, I turned to Carole, and said, 'I want to be part of this man's tremendous plan of touching the world for Christ.'

She nodded her approval. As Palau continued, he revealed how lonely his life as an itinerant evangelist had become.

'I guess the most difficult thing to cope with is that Pat, my wife, and my four boys seldom, if ever, get to go with me in my crusades. We can never afford it.'

The preacher explained that his next meetings were to be in London, and again Pat and the boys would have to stay at home.

I took out my cheque book and began writing out a cheque for three thousand dollars.

'God's been good to us lately,' I whispered to Carole. 'Let's make it possible for Pat and the kids to go with him to England.'

She nodded. 'That would be really nice. If they've got four boys, I know what Pat's been going through.'

I sealed the cheque in an envelope and approached Luis as he got down from the platform.

'Excuse me Mr Palau, but I'm a pastor from Southern California,' I said extending my hand to him. 'God has blessed me with some money from a few inventions I'm involved in and I'd like you to use this money to take your family with you on your next crusade.'

He was taken aback and looked at me strangely. I guess I didn't exactly look as if I was well off.

'Look, sir, I really appreciate it, but I can't take that money from you. I would feel bad.'

'Take it, please. I believe God wants you to have it.' I thrust the envelope into his hand and then left.

When I arrived home, the phone rang. It was Luis Palau sounding very agitated. He had found my number on the cheque.

'Mr Logsdon, I've been thinking, and I just don't see any way I can accept this money from you. I can't let you go without food and clothes just for me. I know what the average pastor earns so I know you can't possibly afford to be as generous as this.'

I was impressed with his reaction, but wouldn't hear of his returning it.

'Look, Mr Palau, I assure you that I *can* afford it. Please have a wonderful time and I'll be praying for you.'

When I put down the receiver and recounted the conversation to Carole, she threw her head back and laughed heartily.

'Duane, maybe there is a purpose for your business after all. Maybe God has given you the 'gift of giving'. The business will provide the funds for you to help Christian ministries like that of Luis Palau. I'm going to make you a promise.'

'What's that?'

'I promise that from this moment on, I'll stop praying for it to go broke. . . .'

# CHAPTER TWENTY-ONE

# Leave or Stay?

The late afternoon sunshine was slanting down towards dusk as I sat in my accountant's office for what I thought would be a routine visit. But it wasn't!

'Duane,' he said seriously, as he sat back in his chair, 'I've just been putting your statement together for Specialty Products and I have to tell you that you've got serious problems.

'The cause is simply *success*. Your business is extremely profitable and because of that you are generating some serious estate problems. You are making so much money that your tax bills will be even more incredible.'

My eyes filled with puzzlement.

'But I thought that was the reason I was in business—to make a profit. Surely that's what it's all about!'

'It is what it's all about, Duane, but the way your company is constituted means that everything will impact upon you and Carole personally. The problem is that you are the sole owners of the corporation and of the patents.'

This high finance was getting beyond me. So I asked my adviser to explain further.

'Duane,' he said, rising up from his chair, 'I know you have told me that you want your business to help finance God's work, but you also have to deal with the legal ramifications of finance and law. You know, render unto Caesar what is Caesar's.

'If you want to continue as you are, you will have to pay extremely high taxes. But if you are willing to make more capital investment, we can limit your tax problems to a degree.'

What a situation to be in! Being penalized for success. People, I knew, had struggled for years to be in the position I was now in. It seemed as if whatever I did in relation to the company worked out well, and more and more profits accrued. Now here was my financial man telling me that I was creating a very bad situation for myself.

I talked with Carole for hours about the predicament we were in.

'I have to ask myself why I am running this business? Is it to make money for money's sake? No, not really. Is it to serve the Lord with my life and all the inventive talent he has given me?

'I also have to ask myself, am I doing that as a pastor? I guess I am to an extent, but not in the same way as I am in the business world.

'Maybe God is telling me to be different, to go contrary to tradition and leave the ministry to go full-time as a businessman. But why?'

Carole turned to me. 'Duane, I wonder if part of the problem is that we both feel terrible guilt about having wealth after many years of struggle. We've always been taught that money and spirituality are on opposite sides of the coin.'

I agreed. 'All I can say is that I feel that a decision needs to be taken soon. Either I stay in the ministry and give up the business or I go in the business world, lock, stock and barrel.'

The next morning, I found myself pacing my office

searching for an answer. 'Lord,' I prayed, 'if you really want me to give up my church pastorate and go full time into the business world, please let me, in return, give you back a million dollars.'

Suddenly, after my time of prayer, I was overwhelmed with the presence of the Lord. I felt God was saying to me, 'I want to make you wealthy beyond your wildest dreams so *you can give it back to me*!

'I want you to forget all your previous concepts and walk through this new experience so others can learn the truth about the biblical concepts of stewardship.'

Then that small voice added, 'Duane, do it for me. The two greatest needs in the Christian world are people and money. I want to use you as a channel to fund my work; I want to prove myself to you and through you. I'm counting on you!

So that was it! God, not me, had made the decision.

I left my office at the company and drove over to my parents' home. They were just sitting down to eat lunch.

'I won't interrupt you, but I just want to share with you that God has told me he is going to bless me with great wealth, and that this is to be used for his work.

'I don't completely understand it all, but I believe that God is talking about Specialty Products.'

My parents smiled in a friendly, but non-committal way and said how wonderful that was, though I don't think they really understood the repercussions of what I had told them.

'Well, son, we'll pray for you that he leads you in all of the details,' said Mother.

Then my father asked, 'What's going to happen at the church, then, son?'

'I don't have the full answer to that yet, Dad. But I'm leaving it to the Lord to work that one out.'

That night, over dinner, I shared all that had happened with Carole.

'Honey,' she observed, 'maybe that is why the Lord stopped the sale of the business on those two occasions we had tried to sell it.'

I agreed. We had agonized for some time over what to do. I had even prayed, 'Lord, if you want me to stay in the pastorate, bring along a buyer for the business.'

Twice we had been within a hair's breadth of closing deals, and then, on each occasion, it had fallen through. I had stipulated that whoever bought Specialty Products had to agree that all royalties from my patents were to be used to fund Christian work. The first prospective buyer had agreed to that, but then pulled out of the deal when the recession hit his group and they no longer had the funds to buy us out. The second possible buyer said point blank they would not agree to my 'strange' stipulation.

I got out my Bible and began reading verse 6 from Proverbs, chapter 3, 'In all thy ways acknowledge him, and he shall direct thy paths.'

As I closed the book, I said to Carole, 'I don't know where all of this is going to lead us, but what I do know is we have to acknowledge him and he will direct us.'

'Let's do that right now.'

We had a time of prayer in which we joined hands and recommitted our lives and the business to God.

As I opened my eyes, I looked at Carole.

'I guess after that I have no alternative but to resign from the pastorate and work full-time in the business.'

'You have no alternative,' she agreed.

John, one of my deacons, looked as if he had been hit by a thunderbolt when I told him the news. 'But Pastor Logsdon we don't want you to resign,' he protested almost plaintively. 'We all love you and Carole so much, don't leave us now.'

I had made the announcement of my resignation from the pulpit on a Sunday morning. It was greeted with gasps of disbelief from throughout the church. Then came the letters pleading with me to stay, and the anguished phone calls. Finally, a few weeks later I asked the congregation to pray with me for a three-week period over what I should do.

'At the end of that time I'll give you a definite answer,' I said, knowing in my heart that I was taking the coward's way out. I knew that God had directed me that morning in my office, but I suppose I felt that perhaps I could continue with the church and the business for a time yet.

'After all,' I reasoned, 'I've been combining the two for nearly seven years now.'

So I agreed to stay. Immediately, however, I began to detect a change in the effectiveness of my ministry. Somehow, I was not having the same impact through my preaching. I was restless in my soul, as if under a conviction that I should not be hanging on. At the end of nine unsettling months, I finally declared to the church that I would be terminating my position as pastor in sixty days.

There was hardly a dry eye in the sanctuary when, on a spring day in 1977, I told them, 'Try as hard as I have, it is obvious that God's plan for our lives here at Anaheim has come to an end. God has another man for you. He had Joshua to fill his place, so let's not linger in the past. Let's instead look forward with renewed hope, for there is still much land for you to possess.'

I knew that there would also be much land for Carole and me to claim for God in our full commitment to him in our new life together.

# CHAPTER TWENTY-TWO

# Something Beautiful for God

The move full time into the business was confirmed as right by the way it boomed even more. The turnover doubled each year. It wasn't exactly an oil well—but not far from it! I began more and more to feel the adrenaline rushing through my veins as I saw a dream taking shape before my very eyes, changing from something nebulous to something tangible.

But as a counter to that excitement, I have to confess that each time I saw the enormous tax bill we were paying, I felt a pang of guilt. So I began to pray about the situation.

'Lord,' I prayed, 'I am really grateful for all the success this represents, but I also know that I am not in this world to make money just for myself or to be a great success.

'I'm here to serve you. This business is dedicated to you and I need to know how I can harness the profits so they can be distributed to deserving Christian ministries.'

Specialty Products had now moved into a beautiful new building in Stanton, a city close to Anaheim, and had built up a national sales organization with about two hundred reps covering the whole of North America.

We were even exporting to Europe, South America and the Middle East. I had registered some twenty patents, both domestic and foreign, and our company had achieved a reputation of being one with 'progressive products for a progressive age' in our industry.

'Lord, I want to harness all of this for you, but I don't know how,' I prayed fervently one day. 'Please show me.'

I had shared my frustration with a business associate. 'Your situation,' he said, scratching his chin, 'sounds similar to that of Dewey and Minna Lockman. They wanted to use their spiritual and material blessings to do something *great* for God's kingdom on earth. Their answer was to develop the Lockman Foundation to promote Christian evangelism and education. God has since used them to present to the world the *Amplified Bible* and the *New American Standard Bible*. Why don't you contact Mr Lockman and see how he did it?'

I telephoned him immediately.

'Mr Lockman,' I said, when he came on the line, 'you don't know me, but my name is Duane Logsdon. I'm almost a neighbour of yours here in California. Well, to come straight to the point, I have a company that markets and manufactures plumbing products, and God has been good to me. I've seen the business multiply into a very healthy corporation in a short period of time.

'It's my desire that this be used for the Lord. I understand you and your family faced a similar problem with your business interests some years ago and you resolved it by forming the Lockman Foundation.'

He said that was true, then indicated he would be delighted to meet me and share any lessons he had learned through his own foundation.

* * *

The comfortable quality of his office made me feel at ease immediately.

'My brother,' said Mr Lockman, a large man with silver-grey hair, as he spread his hands on the desk in front of him, 'I would counsel you not to form a private non-profit foundation. The red tape and the restrictions are unbelievable.'

I swallowed, blinked, and swallowed again. I was totally confused, having thought that this kind of foundation would be the answer for me.

'But,' he continued in a soothing tone as he caught the baffled look on my face, 'there are alternatives. I suggest you find a good lawyer and take another route. He will advise you of the best way.'

I stammered out my thanks. 'Where should I go now?' I wondered.

As I wrestled with this problem, I decided that once again I should not go after the answer, but let God provide it for me in his own good time. That turned out to be a few days after seeing Mr Lockman. A business friend from Dallas telephoned me and told me that a Christian lawyer he knew was going to be in the area in a week.

'Duane,' he said urgently, 'I want you to get together with him. He is an extraordinary Christian with a background in financial law, banking and estate planning. The guy has consulted with Bill Bright of Campus Crusade, the Navigators, Wycliffe Bible Translators, and recently helped Chuck Colson put his prison ministry together in Washington. I've told him about you and he would very much like to meet you and see if he can help.'

The man he was talking about was Doug Keiswetter, a six-foot-two gentle giant, with a warm but thoroughly professional attitude towards life. As I shared with Doug the story of my struggles, the growth of the business, and the problem I faced on how to use this for God, he smiled, his face showing real concern.

'Duane, God is going to do something beautiful with all of this,' he said fervently, his eyes gleaming. 'I'd count it a real privilege to be able to help you develop your plan.'

He began to explain that there could be available to me what was called a 'support foundation' which seemed to completely fit the bill. The plan met the requirements of the Inland Revenue, but he warned it was extremely difficult to obtain.

'Once you receive their approval, it has minimal strings attached and gives you broad latitude as to what you can do with it,' he continued.

'I guess you want to know the difference between a private foundation and a support foundation. Well, a non-profit trust means you can give widely to whomever you wish, while a support foundation means you have to select the categories of ministries that you wish to support. For example, evangelism, Christian education, or overseas missions.

'Then you choose organizations that fall into those categories. If they qualify as non-profit organizations with the Inland Revenue, then you indicate that you will give to such groups in your bylaws.

'The hitch can be that there has to be across-the-board representation, which means you must be a member of the board of the organization you support, or nominate the person who should be your representative, while he, in turn, must have a representative on your board.

'This limits you to a degree but if, in fact, what you wish to do is to support that organization, it doesn't limit you at all.'

'Doug, this looks like the missing piece in the puzzle I have been trying to solve!' I exclaimed.

I warmly shook his hand. My new friend told me he would be happy to work with me on this, but I would also have to use my local lawyer as he would be closer to home.

*     *     *

I never dreamed that one day my business affairs would take me to the Orient. But they did! Carole and I were able to make a business trip to Japan to visit a machine tool company that wanted me to buy more of their products. I was so impressed that I did—one million dollars' worth!

After three weeks away, our boys were delighted to see us back and only too glad to bring us up-to-date on developments in the business.

'Dad, we will have our first showroom on wheels in two weeks,' said Dave, our second son who was now married. He was doing very well as a junior executive member, helping to develop the marketing section of the company. Little did I realize that within one year we would have fifteen mobile showrooms travelling around the country, fully equipped with audio-visuals, colour displays, and photographs of the products.

Dave and our eldest son, Don, now the national sales manager, had worked closely together in this side of the business. We had grown so fast that we were even doing our own in-house work in art graphics, camera work and printing, as well as manufacturing our own products.

Dan, our third boy, was at college. He worked in the business during the summer holidays. Doug, the youngest, also did his bit with us on Saturdays and after school.

It was a thrill for us to be united as a family in this venture.

* * *

Carole and I, and eventually Dan, Don and Doug, moved to a larger home in Fullerton. We could hardly believe the way profits continued to multiply. Strangely, however, I began to feel a real concern about the situation.

I told Carole one day, 'I feel a greater responsibility to God for this business than I did with any of the churches. I know some people will think what I have just said is sacrilegious, but it's true.

'We've got to get this tax situation resolved soon so we can get the business really working for God.'

I also found another problem that weighed me down. It was the feeling of guilt handling such large sums of money. Carole, too, felt conscience-stricken about the situation.

'You know, Duane,' she said, high colour rising up in her cheeks, 'I can't get used to the fact that I now have a really nice home and a car of my own. Yet I know that God has given these blessings to us.' Her hazel eyes looked into mine, and held their gaze.

I then shared with Carole another feeling I had.

'I not only have to come to terms with the feeling of guilt for being wealthy for the first time in my life, but worse than that—I know many of my friends feel I have left the will of God by leaving the ministry. They are saying I did it only because I wanted to become rich.' I let my eyes close tightly for a long moment before continuing.

'Carole, that really hurts, because it isn't true. But still I can understand their problem. After all, they have been taught for years by me that Christians aren't supposed to prosper.

'They will quote that verse I often used from the pulpit: "It is easier for a camel to go through the eye of a needle than for a rich man to enter into the kingdom of God."

'But I now see that verse in another light. You will notice that the Lord says it is *hard*, but he doesn't say it is *impossible*. I'm beginning to realize that it isn't *what you have* that God is concerned about, but *what has you*.'

I opened my Bible again to Matthew 6:33 and read out loud to Carole, 'But seek ye first the kingdom of God, and his righteousness; and all these things shall be added unto you.'

I looked into my wife's deep hazel eyes, 'Carole, I really believe we *are* seeking first the kingdom of God. But I've got another verse for you. Look here in verse 21 it says, "For where your treasure is, there will your heart be also."

'That's the key. What is our treasure? If it is in amassing wealth for its own sake, then we're heading for trouble. But if our treasure is furthering the kingdom of God, well, I know that God is going to bless that.'

I took her hand and affectionately squeezed it.

'Let's get this foundation together and do something really beautiful for God,' I whispered excitedly.

She nodded in agreement, her face flushed with excitement.

# CHAPTER TWENTY-THREE

# Two Million for God

'Pam,' said my lawyer, inclining his head towards his secretary, 'could you see if you can get Overseas Crusades in Santa Clara on the line for Mr Logsdon?' It was the autumn of 1978, and I was at his Los Angeles office drawing up the final details of the Logsdon Foundation and wanted to talk to Luis Palau, who by now was president of this well-known ministry. I wanted Luis to know that I planned to make Overseas Crusades one of the beneficiaries of my foundation.

The Latin evangelist was quickly sparkling down the receiver.

'Duane, you're a hard guy to get hold of. I've been trying to get in touch with you all day. Look, my friend, I've got some news for you. . . .'

Before he could continue, I interrupted his flow.

'Well, Luis, before you go any further, I also have some news for you. I'm in my lawyer's office putting together the articles and bylaws for my foundation. I have decided to name Overseas Crusaders as our worldwide evangelism category. . . .'

I heard the Latin preacher let out a palpable gasp. It was several seconds before he responded. 'Well, that's incredible, Duane, because I have my lawyer here with me in the office putting the paperwork together for a new organization. We are going out on our own and forming the Luis Palau Evangelistic Association and I wanted to know if you would serve on my board.'

He then anticipated my question about why he was moving on.

'Look Duane, it's not a split. We're in total harmony about this. But I feel God is directing us in this severance, that we might be able to reach even more people for Christ.'

This whole conversation was being relayed to all of us via a speaker in the office. I noticed my lawyer and Doug Keiswetter exchanging glances. Then I heard my lawyer exclaim, 'What a coincidence!'

Doug just grinned and said, 'We prefer to call it providence.'

Luis came back on the line. 'Duane, if your documents aren't cast in concrete, could you hold off naming that organization until we get our non-profit clearance in the State of Oregon?'

'Sure, Luis. It is you that I primarily wanted to work with and I really would be happy to be on your board. But why me? I'm just an old country boy, and you work all over the world.'

Luis laughed. 'I thought you were just that when I first met you, but anyone who can build up a business empire like you have can't be all that simple-minded!'

His infectious chuckle continued for a long moment. Then he continued, 'No, seriously, I can see that you are a man of faith and also a very practical person. Someone who can believe with me that God is going to save literally millions of people through this ministry, and also someone who understands business and administration.

'No, brother Duane, I know you are the man for our board.'

It took several long months of negotiations with the State of California to gain our corporation status and then another long battle with the Inland Revenue to qualify as a non-profit organization.

'It makes me laugh that our government should make it so difficult for us to give money away,' I told Carole when they finally recognized the Logsdon Foundation as a bona fide foundation with the sole purpose of disbursing money for Christian work.

I then placed the forty patents that I now owned into the foundation so that all royalties generated from the sales of the different products I had invented would go exclusively into Christian work.

'Carole, at last my move from the pastorate is beginning to make sense,' I told my wife as we happily examined the documents the Inland Revenue had approved for the foundation.

'Now I can really give that one million dollars back to God.'

But God had a different accounting system.

*     *     *

'Duane, I have been going through all your patents and I calculate their minimum worth at this time as $1,500,000,' said a financial advisor who had been working on the papers for me.

'So it looks like you will be able to give back more than you bargained for when you prayed that prayer.'

But then came a real blow. It seemed that now the foundation was functioning, Carole and I were caught up in an impossible situation which threatened all that I had built up.

'But I don't understand,' I told my financial consultant. 'What on earth have we done that is so wrong?'

'Well,' he said, a look of embarrassment sweeping his face, 'you own a corporation and are using part of those profits to fund the foundation.

'The government,' he added, his voice hardening, 'could think that you are using the foundation to avoid paying taxes.'

Stirred up with outrage, I asked, 'Do you mean to say that they think that maybe I could be taking money out of the foundation for myself? But nothing is further from the truth!'

He held up his hands as if to protect himself from my anger.

'You know that, Duane, and so do I, but *they* don't! Unfortunately, not everyone operates with your brand of honesty.'

I was shattered. I looked at him, blinking for a moment, trying to take in what he had just told me. 'Well,' I asked him, 'how are we going to solve this problem?'

He stared at me, his mind searching for an answer.

'The only solution I can see is that you will have to sell the controlling stock in the company.'

'But,' I protested, my eyes filling with great puzzlement, 'if I do that I will lose control.'

'That's the risk you will have to take,' he pointed out with brutal directness. 'You have *no* alternative.'

This was terrible. I felt surprised, hurt and dazed. I had spent many years building up Specialty Products and now he was telling me that I had to hand it over to someone else—just because I had felt led to fund Christian ministries.

'Surely, Lord, this can't be so,' I told him that night as I prayed with Carole. 'I feel I have been caught between a rock and a hard place.

'Here we are,' I continued, an edge of frustration

appearing in my voice, 'trying to give money to your work, and yet we are being treated like criminals. Lord, I don't understand what is going on here, but I do ask you to please solve this problem.'

Carole clasped her hand as I continued my bedside prayer. I had expected her to complain or burst into tears, as in the old days. But this was a different Carole.

'Lord, prove yourself once more to us in this seemingly impossible situation. It is not our desire to amass a fortune for ourselves. It never has been.

'We truly want this money to be used to propagate the gospel in the widest possible way.'

Then the solution came to me like a bolt out of the blue. 'Carole,' I said as we got to our feet, 'the only answer is for us to join with a company that would allow us to continue with our objectives. This would mean they would buy the necessary stock to gain control—at least officially—but would then have to agree to leave complete control and management of the business in my hands.

'We would continue to develop new products and patents that they would never own, and all of those royalties, past, present and future, would continue to belong to the foundation.'

'That means,' said Carole incredulously, 'that they would not be able to buy any property owned by Specialty Products, and the Logsdon family would remain in total control of the company.'

A slight uncertain smile hovered on her lips. 'Only God could pull off a deal like that!'

*  *  *

I went back into the business, not really worrying anymore about what would happen. I somehow knew the Lord would work it out. Several months passed without a sniff of interest from anyone wanting to buy the company on what appeared to be crazy terms. I had told several people that I would only sell the stock on those terms and had received several strange looks which screamed the reaction, 'Duane Logsdon, you must be kidding!'

One person I had shared the situation with was Jerry Siebert, a businessman from Fairfield, Connecticut. I had even forgotten about our talk until he phoned me.

'Hey, Duane, remember our conversation?' he asked enthusiastically, 'I had dinner last night with an executive of the National Chemsearch Corporation in Dallas, Texas. They are wanting to acquire plumbing-related companies. You came to my mind and I told them a little about you.

'I'm calling to see if there is a remote possibility that you would like to talk with one of the three brothers who own the controlling interest of this New York-based corporation.

'They are a fine family with values very similar to yours. Somehow I feel there might be an understanding between you and them. What do you say?'

I told Jerry that I was interested, but my terms would not change. They would have to pay the asking price without negotiation; they could not buy any of our real estate, and they would not own any of the patents. 'All the royalties have to continue to go into the Logsdon Foundation,' I told my colleague.

'And remember, Jerry, my final stipulation is that the Logsdon family stays in full control and manages the company. I know these may sound like unreasonable requirements, but that's my package.'

I expected Jerry to call it off there and then. I know I

had mentioned these terms before, but I was sure he had forgotten them.

'Duane, let me put this to my friends and see what they say. I'll be back to you once I've got their reaction.'

Well, he didn't get back, but instead Lester Levy, one of the brothers, came on the line.

'Mr Logsdon,' he said, 'Jerry has been talking to me about your package and I wondered if we could get together to discuss the possibility of an acquisition by us.'

I told him that if he was interested in flying in from Texas to California, I would be happy to talk to him. He did, and I found him a warm, gracious and sensitive man who seemed to identify with my objectives. Within a matter of three months, all the documentation was signed and sealed and we joined hands with the huge National Chemsearch Corporation, which has offices in some forty-four countries.

Shortly after this, I was in contact with my financial advisor again who was delighted that this sale had gone through so smoothly.

'Duane, I would say that what has happened is nothing short of a miracle,' he enthused. 'And I've got some more interesting news for you. I've been checking on the value of those patents. I reckon they are now worth two million!

'Looks like God's let you give back twice as much as you had planned. And you've only started, Duane. You've only just started.'

# CHAPTER TWENTY-FOUR

# Buried in the Sands

The sun had turned blood orange as it sank behind the stands in an Acapulco baseball stadium. All eyes were on the rough platform illuminated by the stark lights strung up in front of it.

Already perspiration was streaking down Luis Palau's face on the late November day in 1978, as he turned to the 10,000 people packed into the arena and began to speak.

'Esta Noche, cada uno de ustedes tendrá que hacer una decisión,' he began his powerful sermon aimed at the working people of this tourist playground in Mexico.

But I was hearing differently from his native tongue, for Carole and I were plugged into a simultaneous English translation. 'Tonight,' we heard, as Luis tightly clasped in his left hand his huge black leather Bible, 'each one of you here will have to make a decision.'

I felt my heart begin to beat so fast I thought it would come out of my chest as he paced the stage like a caged lion, and preached to this attentive crowd.

Huge insects intermittently dive-bombed him and he swatted them away, then continued with his hour-long message.

'God wants to do something great with your life . . . he wants to change it completely,' he said hoarsely, leaning forward over the edge of the platform and pointing to a man with a droopy moustache in the front row. He shifted uncomfortably in his seat.

Suddenly, Luis asked everyone to stand.

'I'm going to lead you in a prayer and if you want to receive Christ, you pray it after me,' he said. . . . 'You husbands and wives, why not hold hands and do this together. There is nothing more wonderful than when a husband and wife find the Lord together.'

I slipped my hand into Carole's and we said this prayer of commitment along with hundreds of others in the stadium. It was like a recommitment for us. I bit my lower lip and felt tears. It was a profound experience for both of us.

'Carole,' I said, my voice close to cracking, 'there are more people making decisions here for Christ to-night than during the many years of my ministry. Isn't it wonderful that God has allowed us to be a part of this?'

Night after night, the same response occurred and each time I felt joy well up in my whole being.

Often, during the daytime, Carole and I would join with Luis for long walks along the shimmering sands of Acapulco.

'Duane,' asked Luis one day as we moved on ahead of our wives, 'can I ask you a personal question?'

'Sure, what's on your mind?'

'Well, I feel you and Carole are still carrying a terrible burden about leaving your pastorate to concentrate on the business. Is that right?'

I had to admit that that was unfortunately still true. I was experiencing long periods of guilt about what I had done.

'I suppose it's the fact that I haven't yet come to terms with the way God has blessed me,' I said. 'It's such a new experience for me that I suppose I still can't really handle it. And I keep thinking of the criticism that was aimed at me by a few close friends when I finally left the pastorate.'

Luis stopped for a moment and held my gaze. For once his impish humour was missing and he was deadly serious.

'Duane, I want to share something with you that I haven't shared with anyone else.'

I was startled.

'I want to tell you that I believe being in business is an honourable thing. Not something to be ashamed of, as you sometimes seem to think. I also want to tell you that unless I really felt called of God to be an evangelist, I would want to be either a businessman or a lawyer.

'Don't you see that someone in business has such leverage with others to present the claims of Christ. You can now speak to others who have money and power because you have already proved yourself at a high level. These people will listen to you far more than they will a professional minister.'

I had never thought of that before.

'Look, Duane,' he said modulating his voice to suggest that a new thought had just occurred to him, 'why don't you try and attend as many of my crusades around the world as you can. I want to introduce you at breakfasts and lunches for businessmen so you can speak to them,' he said excitedly as his face lit up.

My head was whirling with what I was hearing and what I had seen during this crusade. God had moved me out of a small church background into a worldwide vision for evangelism.

That week was also the first gathering of the new board for the Luis Palau Evangelistic Team. Gathered there were Dr Dick Hillis, Founder of Overseas Crusades; Paul Garza, a highly successful construction contractor from Las Gatos, California and a former missionary to Spain and Portugal; Don Ward, a financial planner; Milton Klausmann, the founder and president of a large aluminium foundry and stamping company. He has since retired. Later joining the board were Dr Ted Engstrom, Executive Director of World Vision, Dr Walter Smyth, Vice President of International Ministries of the Billy Graham Evangelistic Association.

As we sat around the board table for the first time, I felt humbled to be with men of such experience. And it came as quite a shock when Dick Hillis turned his face to me and said, 'Men, I think that Duane Logsdon's experience both in the pastorate and in business administration makes an ideal candidate for vice-chairman for the Palau ministry.'

I felt my jaw suddenly fall open. Others seconded the proposal and before I could protest, Dick asked, 'Would you be willing to assume this responsibility, Duane?'

I made a gurgling sound which was interpreted as yes.

'Right, with that settled,' said Dick, 'let's get on with further business.'

That one simple decision brought me into a closer relationship with Luis Palau than I had ever dreamed of. This amazing man with an incredible burden for evangelism began to phone me from all over the world and share with me the innermost desires of his heart. I warmed so much to him that I felt I could be just as open with him.

I began to devote all my spare time to help put his ministry into shape as far as administration went. I could see that with all the travelling he was doing holding crusades in different parts of the world, he needed an efficiently running machine back in his Portland office.

'Duane,' he told me one day, 'I really believe that the Lord has brought you into my life to help me fulfil the dreams and visions I have for this ministry.'

Whenever I was able to, I would attend his crusades and have the privilege of sharing my story with businessmen and others in Bellingham, Washington; Newcastle, Australia; and Leeds, England.

Although I threw myself into this new challenge, Luis could still see that Carole and I were still not completely free of our burden of guilt for leaving the pastorate.

On the way back from Australia, Luis, Pat and Carole and I stopped off for a short break on the beautiful island of Tahiti in French Polynesia.

'Duane, I still see *the* cloud,' Luis told me as we walked along the sun-drenched beach to the sound of waves hitting the shores.

For a long moment I stopped and just stared at him. His keen eyes bored into mine. Then the full impact of his words became clear.

'Yes, you're right. I feel a dead, heavy weight inside of me. I suppose I really need to bury them in the sands of Tahiti. But it's not easy.'

We continued our walk and both opened up about our dreams for worldwide evangelism and the goals of the Palau team.

'Duane, look at it this way. If you hadn't heeded God's call to go full time into business, you would still be ministering to a few hundred people in Anaheim. Now there's nothing wrong with that, but I believe God's called you for even greater things than that. I see you as a vital part of this machinery to reach millions of people, whole nations, even presidents, for Christ. I believe also that your example can encourage other businessmen to believe God for great things. You are a visual aid that they can look at and learn from.

'I know that you once prayed, "Lord, let me give you a million dollars." I also know that you and Carole agonized for many months over the issues involved in the change. You both bled spiritually. But now you have come out with solid answers.'

Carole and Pat had by now caught up with us.

'Duane,' said Carole, her eyes alive and sparkling, 'this all seems a long way from Mount Vernon. But, isn't it wonderful what God has done!'

I nodded my head excitedly as she smiled and took my arm.

'Yes,' I replied, 'to be truthful I have to admit that, for a time, when God took me out of the pulpit, I felt short-changed. I still held onto the idea that ministering was wrapped up in pastoring only.

'But God knew better. I now really feel that ministering is having an impact on the lives of all the people we make contact with. Now, through all that has happened, God has given us the privilege of touching millions through the ministry of giving.

'You know,' I chuckled as the three looked on, 'I asked the Lord if I could give him *one* million dollars! Oh, me of little faith . . .!'

# Where He Leads

**by John Graham**
*with Richard Schneider*

This is the true story of what happened when one man was prepared to give up everything for God – even his home and a successful medical practice. To many, John Graham appeared unwise, even foolish. But little by little he was learning that it is always best to follow the prompting of the Holy Spirit, no matter where He leads. And he discovered that, as he obeyed in matters large and small, God gave abundant riches in return.

> *'I knew I loved God. But did I obey Him in everything? Of course not; sometimes it was just too difficult, at other times impractical and, more often than not, just too embarrassing.*
>
> *But John Graham learned to obey. And he found himself achieving things of which he had never dreamed.*
>
> *John's story has changed my life.*
> *It may well change yours.'*

Richard Schneider
*Co-author of*
I DARED TO CALL HIM FATHER

*Kingsway Publications*

# Too Soon to Die

## by Nick Pirovolos with William Proctor

*'I glanced in my rearview mirror and saw a couple of guys in a car just behind us. Something didn't look quite right. I shouted, "Something's up!" and put my foot down. Just as well. One of the guys on our tail stuck a pistol out of his window and started firing.*

*Things were happening so fast there was no time to think. We were barrelling along at 115 miles an hour, sometimes on the wrong side of the road, sometimes on the pavement. The gunmen shot my rear tyre. I went into a spin and slammed into a parked car. I was knocked half senseless. Out of the corner of my eye I saw the two hit men walking towards me. One of them yanked my car door open, stuck his gun in my face, and pulled the trigger...'*

From immigrant boy to fearless criminal, Nick the Greek diced with death. He knew what it was to survive on the streets.

Going to prison didn't change him much—until one night mean, hard Nick the Greek learned how to cry. Jesus Christ had broken into his life. From now on, inside or outside the prison walls, he was determined that *everyone* should hear his hard-hitting gospel message...

*Kingsway Publications*

# Second Chance

## by Darla Milne

Israel Narvaez was tough: as president of the MauMaus street gang in New York City during the late fifties, he and his vice-president Nicky Cruz felt they could out-fight any group — the Angels, the Chaplains, the Viceroys.

But one day Nicky had his life turned around, all because of a bold young preacher named Dave Wilkerson, who dared to walk their streets and preach Christ. Narvaez, too, said ''yes'' to Christ at a rally, but before he could get his roots down into the Christian faith, a broken promise led him into a fateful detour — one that was to cost him several bitter years in prison on a murder rap.

This book tells the gripping story of how Israel Narvaez got a second chance at life. Today he is a minister of the gospel.

Kingsway Publications

# I Dared to Call Him Father


**by Bilquis Sheikh**
*with Richard Schneider*


This is a book for everyone who wonders what would happen if he gave himself to God completely. 'Will he really fulfil his promises to take care of me — to protect me under all conditions?'

It is the true story of Bilquis Sheikh, a Pakistani woman of noble birth who faced such questions at the crossroads of her life. After she was left by her husband (a high-ranking government official), she retreated to her family estate to find peace and live out her days in quiet luxury. But the deep-down peace she sought eluded her. Searching in the Koran, she found many references to the prophet Jesus. Out of curiosity, she turned to the pages of the Christian Bible.

Then her life turned upside down as a series of strange dreams launched her on a quest that would consume her heart, mind and soul.

*Kingsway Publications*